The *Guanxi* of Relational International Theory

T0373632

This book offers a relational theory of International Relations (IR). To show the ways in which the relationality is foreshadowed in IR conversations, it makes the following three points:

1   it recovers a mode of IR theorizing as itinerant translation;
2   it deploys the concept and practices of *guanxi* (employed here as a heuristic device revealing the infinite capacity of international interactions to create and construct multiple worlds) to uncover the outlines of a relational IR theorizing; and
3   it demonstrates that relational theorizing is at the core of projects for worlding IR.

By engaging with the phenomenon of relationality, Emilian Kavalski invokes the complexity of possible worlds and demonstrates new possibilities for powerful ethical-political innovations in IR theorizing. Thus, relational IR theorizing emerges as an optic which both acknowledges the agency of 'others' in the context of myriad interpretative intersections of people, powers, and environments (as well as their complex histories, cultures, and agency) and stimulates awareness of the dynamically intertwined contingencies through which meanings are generated contingently through interactions in communities of practice.

    The book will have a strong appeal to the broad academic readership in Asian Studies, Political Science, Comparative Politics, International Relations theory, and students and scholars of non-/post-Western International Relations and non-/post-Western Political Thought.

Emilian Kavalski is Associate Professor of Global Studies at the Institute for Social Justice, Australian Catholic University. Emilian's research focusses on post-colonial literature, European politics, International Theory, Asian affairs, and the post-humanities.

Rethinking Asia and International Relations
Series Editor – Emilian Kavalski, Australian Catholic
University (Sydney)

For a full list of titles in this series, please visit www.routledge.com/
Rethinking-Asia-and-International-Relations/book-series/ASHSER1384

This series seeks to provide thoughtful consideration both of the growing
prominence of Asian actors on the global stage and the changes in the study
and practice of world affairs that they provoke. It intends to offer a comprehensive parallel assessment of the full spectrum of Asian states, organisa-
tions, and regions and their impact on the dynamics of global politics.

The series seeks to encourage conversation on:

- what rules, norms, and strategic cultures are likely to dominate international life in the 'Asian Century';
- how will global problems be reframed and addressed by a 'rising Asia';
- which institutions, actors, and states are likely to provide leadership
  during such 'shifts to the East';
- whether there is something distinctly 'Asian' about the emerging patterns of global politics.

Such comprehensive engagement not only aims to offer a critical assessment
of the actual and prospective roles of Asian actors, but also seeks to rethink
the concepts, practices, and frameworks of analysis of world politics.

This series invites proposals for interdisciplinary research monographs
undertaking comparative studies of Asian actors and their impact on the
current patterns and likely future trajectories of international relations. Fur-
thermore, it offers a platform for pioneering explorations of the ongoing
transformations in global politics as a result of Asia's increasing centrality
to the patterns and practices of world affairs.

Forthcoming titles

The *Guanxi* of Relational International Theory
Emilian Kavalski

The *Guanxi* of Relational International Theory

Emilian Kavalski

LONDON AND NEW YORK

First published 2018
by Routledge
2 Park Square, Milton Park, Abingdon, Oxon OX14 4RN

and by Routledge
605 Third Avenue, New York, NY 10017

First issued in paperback 2021

Routledge is an imprint of the Taylor & Francis Group, an informa business

British Library Cataloguing-in-Publication Data
A catalogue record for this book is available from the British
Library

Library of Congress Cataloging-in-Publication Data
A catalog record for this book has been requested

ISBN 13: 978-1-03-209628-5 (pbk)
ISBN 13: 978-1-138-08878-8 (hbk)

Typeset in Times New Roman
by Apex CoVantage, LLC

Contents

Acknowledgements

Monographs are usually a labour of love. This one is not! Instead, this book gratifies the demands imposed on academic performance in Australia. In all fairness, this book is an article force-fed into obesity so that it can be deemed valuable by the Antipodean branch of neoliberal governmentality! Although an outcome of necessity rather than love, the completion of this project would have not been possible without the support of so many. It is their example, encouragement, and friendship that help me to keep on hoping (despite all the gathering darkness).

Versions of the main argument were presented at a number of meetings, and I would like to thank the participants and organizers for their engagement and critical feedback. At the First Afrasian Symposium, 'Beyond "West" and "Rest": A Critical Inquiry into the Dichotomized Ontology of International Relations' (27 February 2016, Ryukoku University, Japan): special thanks are due to Kosuke Shimizu and Ching-Chang Chen for welcoming me to this event, as well as to Pinar Bilgin, L.H.M. Ling, Takashi Inoguchi, Yong-Soo Eun, and Kelvin Cheung. At the workshop, 'Theorising China's Rise in and beyond International Relations' (31 March 2016, Deakin University, Australia): Chengxin Pan (for his continuous generosity and collaboration), John Agnew, Shahran Akbarzadeh, Barry Buzan, Baogang He, Wang Jisi, Evelyn Goh, Chih-yu Shih, See Seng Tan, and Bin Yu. At the 12th Lodz East Asia Meeting (2–3 June 2016, University of Łódź, Poland): Dominik Mierzejewski, Thomas Gold, Marcin Grabowski, Viktor Eszterhai, Noémi Eszterhainé Szőke, and Mirosław Michał Sadowski. At the workshop, 'History and Strategy in East Asia: A Critical Appraisal' (21 October 2016, Yonsei University, Korea): Jungmin Seo (for his generous hospitality), Hun Joon Kim, Xiangfeng Yang, Lindsay Black, Yong Wook Lee, Sang Joon Kim, Hitomi Koyama, Sung Kyung Kim, and Young Hoon Song. At the workshop, 'Futures of Global Relations' (16–17 May 2017, Lancaster University, UK): Astrid H.M. Nordin (for including me in the conversations), Raoul Bunskoek, Huang Chiung-chiu, Yihjye

(Jay) Hwang, Patrick Thaddeus Jackson, Mari Nakamura, Daniel H. Nexon, Graham M. Smith, David Tyfield, Emma Williams, and Marysia Zalewski. At the Sydney School for Critical Social Thought (25 May 2017, Institute for Social Justice, Australia): Jeannie Morefield (for her thoughtful and generous response), Linda Martin Alcoff, Paul Apostolidis, Rajeev Bhargava, Akeel Bilgrami, Joseph Carens, Romand Coles, Costas Douzinas, Naser Ghobadzadeh, Paula Gleeson, Kiran Grewal, Lia Haro, Nikolas Kompridis, Jeanne Morefield, Jennifer Nedelsky, Jacqueline Rose, Lisa Tarantino, and Allison Weir.

Although he participated at/organized many of the previously listed events, Young Chul Cho seems to never tire of my complaints and has been providing respite, refuge, and support on so many occasions even though his own circumstances were/are oftentimes worse than mine. Tsai Tung-Chieh and Tony Tai-Ting Liu have gone above and beyond to ensure that I'm always 'welcome to the Chungle' and to demonstrate their care. Special thanks are also owed to Brett Bowden, Barthélémy Courmont, Emel Pralar Dal, Bart Dessein, Niv Horesh, Chris Ogden, Tanguy Struye de Swielande, Yoneyuki Sugita, Dorothée Vandamme, David Walton, Thomas Wilkins, Jingdong Yuan, and Faruk Yalvaç. I am also grateful to my editors at Routledge, Rob Sorsby and Claire Maloney for their patience and support. The completion of this manuscript was made possible by a generous grant from the Taiwan Fellowship program.

Finally, I need to thank Raycho Kavalski, Magdalena Zolkos, baby Sava and Cyril (who will always be my baby) for reminding me that relationality is much more than just this. For this and so much more, I love you!

Introduction

The Columbus syndrome
of international relations

Introduction

International relations (IR) theory suffers from a Columbus syndrome. The 1492 voyage of Christopher Columbus set in motion the period of European conquest – often referred to in Western scholarship as the 'age of discovery' and by indigenous communities around the world as a period of 'invasion and dispossession'. However, Columbus himself failed to recognize the newness of the 'New World' that he supposedly discovered. It is well known that he did not think that he had reached a new continent, but that he had hit the eastern shores of Asia. More importantly, in the context of the current discussion, his encounter with the various Amerindian peoples was effectively prevented by his own cultural, religious, and ideological prejudices. It might appear puzzling today, but Columbus refused to recognize that the Amerindians spoke a different language from him. Instead, he merely assumed that the indigenous populations were unable to speak. For this reason, he took several Amerindians to teach them how to speak (and by that he meant to speak a European language). Thus,

> Columbus's failure to recognize the diversity of languages permits him, when he confronts a foreign tongue, only two possible, and complementary, forms of behaviour: *to acknowledge it as a language but to refuse to believe it is different; or to acknowledge its difference but to refuse to admit it is a language.*
>
> (Todorov 1982: 30; emphasis added)

In this respect, Columbus 'knows in advance what he will find' (Todorov 1982: 17) and acknowledges only the things that fits his preconceived model, while ignoring all the aspects that were incongruent.

My claim is that the IR mainstream (and I am aware that this is an overgeneralization) suffers from a similar condition to that of Columbus (which goes beyond the mere cognitive dissonance of the discipline). Thus, when it encounters 'other' concepts, practices, and experience of the 'international', IR more often than not reverts to the prism of its Columbus syndrome: either it recognizes them as narratives about world politics but does not acknowledge that they are different or it acknowledges that they are different but refuses to admit that they are part of IR (thereby relegating them to fields such as cultural studies, area studies, anthropology, etc.). In either case, the IR mainstream tends to prioritize ontologies of separation rather than connectedness – and this is the real source of its Columbus syndrome. Such a tendency presages a 'significant epistemic shift' in IR that espouses 'positivistic principals' and prescribes 'value neutrality' (Hobson 2012: 185). This, however, only 'sublimated' the Columbus syndrome 'rather than exorcise[d] it' (Hobson 2012: 214). In response to this condition, this book proposes a relational theory of IR drawing on the concept and practices of *guanxi*.

As Jacques Barsun presciently anticipated: 'To see ourselves as others see us is a rare and valuable gift, without a doubt. But in international relations what is still rarer and far more useful is to see others as they see themselves' (Barsun 1965: 426). Since the late 1990s, the literature on IR has witnessed a growing number of contributions to what might be called a 'relational turn' in the discipline[1]; yet none of them has been able to suggest what a relational theory of IR would look like. This book proposes such a relational theory. Although relationality has been mentioned in the IR literature earlier, the relational turn in international relations has gradually been growing into prominence since the seminal article by Patrick Thaddeus Jackson and Daniel H. Nexon (1999). Their proposition is that the mainstream has tended to focus on actors (regardless of whether they are state, non-state, or transnational) at the expense of the very relations that constitute both these actors and global life. The premise of the relational turn is fairly straightforward – different kinds of social contexts (both temporal and spatial) engender different forms of international order. For instance, the Sino-American relationship in Northeast Asia is quite different from the Sino-American interactions in the South China Sea (or other global locales, as well as over time). The point that the contributors to the relational turn make is that the focus on discrete transactions abstracted from the context in which they take place distorts both the nature of the particular transactions and the character of the broader pattern of relations. The proponents of the relational turn advocate sidelining the usual preoccupation with the 'levels of analysis' by immersing the study and practice of IR in the 'connectedness across diversities' between all 'the constituents of the globe' (Shahi and Ascione 2016: 313–334).

While undertaking a much-needed assessment of two of the main branches of the 'larger family of *relational social theory*' (Jackson and Nexon 2017: 1;

emphasis in original) – its so-called Anglophone and Sinophone clans – the primary aim of this book is to offer a relational theory of IR that transcends such bifurcations. It has to be stated at the outset that the labels of Anglophone and Sinophone are deployed here as operational shorthand for framing the argument. They should not be misunderstood as ascriptions of something essentially Western or Chinese about either of these respective approaches; in fact, this project is quite critical of any such attempt to develop 'national' schools or approaches to IR (Cho 2015; Hobson 2004, 2012; Ling 2015). As it will become apparent, this book draws attention to the porousness and unpredictability of global life – both Western and non-Western – and the messy and contingent interactions that permeate and constitute both. This project affiliates itself with ongoing *worlding* of IR (Agathangelou and Ling 2009; Chan et al. 2001; Shilliam 2010). On the one hand, such worlding intends to pluralize disciplinary inquiry by engaging previously excluded alternatives for thinking and doing world politics that have been forged both historically and in contemporary times by scholars, practitioners, and activists. On the other hand, such worlding offers productive openings to bring into a meaningful conversation a wide range of cosmologies, power relations, and vulnerabilities than are typically accounted for by the narratives of IR.

Having said that, the reference to Anglophone and Sinophone versions of the relational turn in IR also acknowledges that the contributors to these strands tend to identify with (and often assert such) division as a marker of the different cultural resources on which they draw. Thus, those in the Anglophone camp of the relational turn primarily draw on the Eurocentric 'canon' of IR (and oftentimes disregard or marginalize – both explicitly and implicitly – 'other' traditions), whereas those in the Sinophone one tend to focus on Chinese ideas at the expense of taking relevance to existing Western concerns. The contention is that the current state of the art on the relational turn has so far failed to transcend the separation between the Western and the Chinese strands and bring them to meaningful conversation. This book suggests that a genuinely *relational IR* theorizing is neither Sinocentric nor Eurocentric, but cultivated from the convivial, yet dissonant, cross-pollination of values, narratives, and practices in the study of world affairs. The claim is that recent attempts to bring the Anglophone and Sinophone strands of the relational turn in IR into conversation have so far failed to transcend the bifurcating metanarrative of the mainstream, let alone account for the multiple intersections permeating the strategic search for relations with others. Before proceeding further, the following sections of this introductory chapter outline the analytical framework of the book and detail the development of the argument in the following chapters.

The analytical framework of the book

The intention of this book is neither to treat nor perceive the Anglophone and Sinophone (as well as other linguistic traditions) as closed systems that are impermeable and separate from one another, but as interrelated and constantly intermingling. Plurality is always already built into those traditions. Sometimes they grow distant, sometimes they draw closer together; sometimes they are in conflict, sometimes they live in harmony, and sometimes they fuse with one another. As it has already been indicated, to assist the disclosure of the ways in which the affordances of relationality are foreshadowed in the current conversations on the relational turn in IR, the projected manuscript enlists the Chinese concept of *guanxi*. The necessary caveat is that *guanxi* is deployed here as a heuristic device revealing the infinite capacity of (international) interactions to create and construct multiple worlds rather than as a term illustrating the actual practices of Chinese foreign policy. Although such connections are clearly there (especially in places like Central Asia and in initiatives such as the 'One Belt, One Road' policy), the point here is to construct an epistemically and ontologically relational theory of IR made possible by the encounter with *guanxi*. In other words, this is not a book about the international practices of China, but about the ways in which Chinese concepts – such as *guanxi* – can aid the 'uncovery'[2] of alternative and, especially, relational modes of IR theorizing. Drawing on the ideational and praxiological repositories of *guanxi*, the projected book analyzes and amplifies the relationality both of global life and the realms of IR. The proposition is that such an endeavor discloses new possibilities for powerful ethical-political innovations in IR theorizing.

To achieve its aims, this book will undertake three distinct yet mutually reinforcing moves: (1) it recovers a mode of IR theorizing as itinerant translation; (2) it uses the concept and practices of *guanxi* to uncover the outlines of a relational IR theorizing; and (3) it demonstrates that relational IR theory is at the core of projects for worlding IR.

International theory as itinerant translation

In the mid-nineteenth century, a Chinese interpreter of the Bible acknowledged that

> having perused the present translation of the scriptures in Chinese, I find it exceedingly verbose, containing much foreign phraseology, so contrary to the usual style of our books that the Chinese cannot thoroughly understand the meaning. It ought to be known that, in the Chinese, phrases have a certain order, and characters a definite application,

which cannot be departed from with propriety . . . Now it appears to me, that *the present version is in Chinese words, but in many respects arranged according to the English idiom.* In a translation, the sense ought certainly to be given, according to the original; but the style should be conformable to native models: thus everyone will take up the book with pleasure, and read it with profit.
(Chooh Tih-Lang quoted in Medhurst 1838: 529; emphasis added)

For me, this statement is reflective of IR's Columbus syndrome. In this respect, the aim of this project is to recover a mode of IR theorizing that it calls 'itinerant translation'. At its most basic, itinerant translation draws on a tradition of intellectual wandering, peregrination, and trespassing which does not subscribe to linear logics of detachment, coherence, and parsimony. It is a normative journey of fusion, exchange, dialogue, and contestation which does not privilege any site or mode of knowledge production nor demand impartiality and objectivity from the theorist. In fact, theorists are creative agents (1) facilitating the interaction between different bodies and cultures of knowledge; (2) translating and arranging the material; and (3) providing openings to worlds otherwise unthinkable (even if unnerving). Thus, by demonstrating that there is more than one way of seeing, hearing, and responding, theorizing as itinerant translation discloses the world as a multiversal space where alternative realities can and do coexist and have done so for quite some time. As such, itinerant translation mandates tolerance of at least as much diversity, inconsistency, and contradictions, as evident in the complex entanglements of the worlds being narrated (Krippendorf 2000: 1–19).[3] At the same time, it reminds IR that theorizing is a sense-making process which is simultaneously quite distinct from 'the reality of international practice' and poignantly transactional at the very level of 'the observer' and 'the observed' – namely, IR theories are not objective representations of the world, but 'artistic creations, shaped by the taste and style of a single hand' (Waltz 1979: 68).

Thus, although a radical endeavour, the positioning of IR theory as a relational construct also acts as a reminder of the itinerant and translational nature of theorizing. Such theorizing draws on the etymology of the term theory. In its Greek original, one of the meanings of the word *theoria* referred to 'a journey or a pilgrimage', involving a willingness to travel to foreign locales that can then simultaneously inform and transform the 'home' of the traveller (Nightingale 2004: 4–9). Equally significantly, by providing a potent form of social interactions, the itinerant performativity of such theoretical travels played an important role in shaping international relations at the time by providing opportunities for 'constant reframing and reconfigurations of participants towards each other', which allowed the ancient Greeks to 'imagine and exploit forms of inter-*polis* contact' (Kowalzig 2005: 41–72). By extension – as the statement by the nineteenth-century Chinese interpreter Chooh Tih-Lang suggests at the start of this section – theorizing becomes a relational process of irruptive translation that brings into dialogue the form and substance of the languages and experiences of diverse and infinitely complex worlds. It belies an openness to the other which does not merely intertwine identity and alterity, but makes 'the act of translating a process of continuous dislocation' (Costa 2013: 79). Chooh Tih-Lang's assertion of the transactional nature of translation seems to echo the proposition of the tenth-century Buddhist monk Zan Ning that ' "to translate" means "to exchange", that is to say, take what one has in exchange for what one does not have' (quoted in Cheung 2010: 34). Yet in lieu of the messiness and dislocation associated with such itinerant translation, IR theory seems to recognize 'other' languages and narratives of theory building only to the extent that they can be '*arranged according to the English idiom*'. As a result, the realties, complexities, and dynamism of global life are reduced to fit pre-scripted storylines (Querejazu 2016: 8; Shimizu 2013: 2).

Such an endeavour should resonate with much of what the mainstream already admits theorizing in IR is about – namely, the identification, observation, explanation, and understanding of patterns by looking at the record of what happens when international actors come together in space and time. Thus, it is creativity and improvisation rather than the provision of prescriptive or proscriptive solutions that promise to heal the habits of control, manipulation, and exploitation associated with IR's insistence on the separation between subject and object, knower and known, self and other, mind and matter (Kavalski 2018a). Although the insistence that IR theory is a relational construct distinct from 'the reality of international practice' might appear radical to some, it merely draws attention to the itinerant and translational nature of theorizing (Kavalski et al. 2018). Such framing betrays the complex, eclectic, and non-objective blend of cultural universals and culturally specific patterns of social relations underpinning the encounter with global life. The point is that IR cannot continue to ignore the flexibilities, contingencies, and transformative possibilities engendered by the encounter with other lifeworlds and knowledges so that it can sustain the integrity of an outlook committed to the analysis of discrete atomistic actors whose behaviour is predetermined by the distribution and balance of power. In the book, itinerant translation also uncovers (and reflects upon) the struggle to move beyond a mode of thinking governed by the logic of binary oppositions and to find a way of theorizing without being silenced by the hegemonic strength of any master narrative, on the one hand, and without being trapped in essentializing the 'Chineseness' and/or 'Westerness' of relationality, on the other. No culture, no tradition, no person can on their own provide a full idea of what global life is. The modality of itinerant translation facilitates the dialogical encounter *with* and *between* pluralities of different perspectives and experiences.

Guanxi *and the relational turn in international relations*

Although one of the terms that make the Chinese phrase for international relations (*guoji guanxi*), *guanxi* has remained occluded from the disclosure of an ontologically and epistemically *relational IR*. The point here is that in contrast to the dualistic bifurcations that dominate IR imaginaries, the concept of *guanxi* illuminates that the complex patterns of global life resonate with the fragility, fluidity, and mutuality of global interactions, rather than the static and spatial arrangements implicit in the fetishized currency of self–other/centre–periphery/hegemon–challenger models underpinning the binary metanarratives of IR. This is a major departure from the current state of the art on relationality in IR, where the so-called 'relational turn' has been deployed mainly to inform the strategic culture – especially its bilateral and multilateral outlook – of different international actors. Thus, rather than looking at dyadic sets of relations as well as the identities and capacity of individual actors, the engagement with the concept of *guanxi* inheres an IR pivoted on webs of figurations intertwined by a conscious and strategic search for relations with others. As Chih-yu Shih notes, 'because most IR theories laude competition, estrangement, and defence, *non-competitive relations* external to balance of power, desire for status, or enforcement of norms in an imagined anarchy *are, by and large, left unexplained*' (Shih 2016: 2; emphasis added). The critical contribution of these endeavours is the development of a potential that has remained latent in both the Anglophone and Sinophone contributions to the relational turn in IR – namely, the entanglement with the complexity paradigm in the philosophy of science and IR in particular.

Thus, relations are not only at the heart of explaining and understanding the world, but also are central to its observation and encounter.[4] The epistemic verso of a *relational IR* is therefore about the cultivation of attentiveness to the self-organizing, shifting, and historically and geographically contingent realities of the global life we inhabit. Such attentiveness will undoubtedly make the realms of IR research messy, yet would assist with the recovery of a disposition to encounter (and respond to) currents, trends, and voices that are uncomfortable and are not easily digestible by established paradigms. In short, a *relational IR* involves an utterly otherwise than neutral, invisible, and uncommitted mode of inquiry. At the same time, it is this very receptivity of a relational IR that holds the promise for *working about* and *working with* the 'edges of radical unusual possibilities' (Coles 2016: 53). Thus, engaging with and listening curiously and provocatively to the phenomenon of *guanxi* invokes the complexity of possible worlds uncovered by relational IR theorizing. Incurred in the interaction via a metaphor of kinship, this type of relationality engenders a process of constant adaptation (Shih 2016: 5–6). Theorizing in this setting is not about the provision of knowledge in the sense that we have since the Enlightenment – rather, it is about forming than purely informing; it is about the art of living than abstract thought. In other words, relational knowledge production is incoherent and socially mediated – just like global life. Relational theorizing as the concept and practices of *guanxi* suggest is about knowledge that is embedded in repertoires of interaction.

The necessary caveat is that the book focuses on the ideal type inherent in the *guanxi* model of relationality rather than its manifestation in the actual practices of Chinese foreign policy.[5] Although such connections are clearly there, the point here is to disclose an epistemically and ontologically relational IR made possible by the encounter with *guanxi*. In other words, this is a manuscript not about the international practices of China, but about the ways in which Chinese concepts – such as *guanxi* – can assist the disclosure of alternative and, especially relational, modes of IR. Postcolonial scholars have long bemoaned this unending demand to constantly qualify, bracket, and signpost their engagement with non-Western ideas, whereas the tendency to promote Western concepts – such as sovereignty, democracy, and human rights – in the abstract (not least because of their presumed universalism) has never seemed to trouble 'Eurocentric IR' and in fact has been 'fetishized' in the narratives of its interlocutors (Chowdhry 2007: 106).[6] Thus, in the view of Western modernity and rationality, reality and its phenomena are assumed to be abstract and generalizable wholes, which are singular, out there, and defined; consequently,

> the anxiety against relativism is one of the most prevailing forces for gatekeeping in IR. It becomes the cause of a constant blackmail: in dichotomous thinking, we only get to choose between one pole or the other, *never both, never something else.*
>
> (Querejazu 2016: 7; emphasis added)

It is perhaps this feature of Anglophone IR that bespeaks its Columbus syndrome when it comes to the encounter with non-Anglo terms – to paraphrase from a different context, it belies IR's

> fairly simplistic faith in the omnilateral superiority of the West; [its] belief that evolution as it took place in Europe is the only evolution

0

possible, the only kind desirable, the kind the whole world must undergo; to sum up, [its] rarely avowed but real belief in civilization with a capital C and progress with a capital P (as evidenced by [IR's] hostility to what [it] disdainfully call 'cultural relativism').

(Césaire [1956] 2010: 149)

Although this book does not suggest that post-Western IRs have to engage in reverse 'deflection',[7] it insists that IR can have (and, in fact, sorely needs) a culturally attuned and contextually verdant engagement with ideas independent of the practices of the governments that administer the territories and societies from which such ideas originate.

Relational IR theory and worlding IR beyond the Eurocentric frame

Bringing in concepts such as *guanxi* assists with accounting for the complex, eclectic, and non-objective blend between cultural universals and culturally specific patterns of social interaction underpinning the ratiocination of post-Western IR (Chen 2011; Eun 2016). Many have written insightfully and exhaustively about the totalizing universalism of mainstream IR and its suppression of the flexibilities, contingencies, and transformative possibilities permeating global life. The critical contribution of the proposed book project is that relationality has become a defining feature of post-Western IR theory building. It seems few today would dispute that the disciplinary inquiry of IR is indelibly marked by the 'colonial signs' of its Eurocentric makeup. Not only that, but the 'apple pie' flavour that IR acquired in the context of its Cold War transformation into an 'American social science' seems to have made the discipline even more inimical towards encounters with the various non-Western others that its outlook consciously occludes. In an attempt to trouble the juxtapositions of temporal and geographical difference that still seem to stump any IR alternative prefixed by a 'non-' or a 'post-', this project posits the centrality of relationality as a distinguishing feature of all such projects. In this setting, the relationality lens helps outline the contested terrain of post-Western IR as a space for dialogical learning, which encourages engagement with the possibilities afforded by the interactions of multiple worlds and privileges the experiences and narratives of neither of them.

The 'itinerant translation' mode of theorizing made possible through the entanglement with the concept and practices of *guanxi* allows for building solidarity between like-minded projects targeting the silencing, hegemony, patriarchy, and violence of the mainstream by treating them as second-order aspects deriving from a first-order problematique – IR's poignant ontological and epistemic *lack of relationality*. It is the very denial of relationality (first-order issue) that perpetuates the imperial, patriarchal, and racist attitudes (second-order issues) of IR. It is in this vein that the attack on the latter that so much of critical, feminist, and postcolonial theorizing undertakes overlooks the very condition of its possibility – the lack of relationality in IR. What this means is that the IR mainstream has been dominated by an atomistic understanding of global life which prioritizes fixed units of analysis (nation-states) and their discrete dyadic interactions (conflict/balancing in the context of anarchy). As a result, IR theories remain invariably immersed in issues of competition, conflict, and defence. Yet at no point is the option of a non-competitive sociability infused with mutuality, self-restraint, and the contingent opportunities inherent in the encounter with the other acknowledged in this narrative.

Relational modes of theorizing offer practices, figurations, and optics for thinking through the paradoxes of modernity; the limits of knowledge (and its production); and the contingency of global life. A *relational IR theorizing* – which is post-Western in the sense that it does not treat the West and the non-West as discrete and disconnected homogenous opposites, but as intertwined and mutually constitutive webs of interactions – proposes a molecular outlook whose unit of analysis is relations (rather than actors) and their multiple triadic dynamics (which open numerous and numinous points of and possibilities for interaction). Such encounters and experiences challenge us – both as individuals and as scholars – as well as global IR theory (in its Anglophone, Sinophone, and other variants), to confront realities which are uncomfortable and which we might not want to confront. The attentiveness to relationality can make a powerful case for envisoning global life and creating ethical openings for reimagining the complex webs of entanglements and encounters with others beyond the divisiveness and violence suffusing current domestic, national, and world politics.

Outline of the book

The chapters included in this book have been carefully crafted to illuminate a relational theory of IR with the help of the concept and practices of *guanxi*. The intention of such contribution to the 'relational turn' in the discipline is to remind IR that global life resonates with fragility, fluidity, and mutuality. The reciprocity and entanglements of these interactions inhere an IR pivoted on webs of figurations intertwined by the constant and strategic pursuit of relations with others. Such framing invokes the 'international' not merely as a stage for world affairs, but as *global life* – a relational entanglement brimming with the coexistence of multiple 'worlds', 'domains', 'projects', and 'texts' of ongoing and overlapping interconnections (Kavalski 2018b).

At the beginning of this journey of healing IR from its Columbus syndrome is the itinerant translation of the Congress of Vienna. The claim is that the standard narrative of the Congress in IR furnishes the foundation stone for the substantialist and Eurocentric worldview of the discipline. During nine months, from November 1814 to June 1815, the participants at the Congress 'waltzed' and 'feasted' their way to an agreement on the post-Napoleonic international order. However, rather than a complex and nuanced 'dance', IR narrates the experience of the Congress through the metaphor of a formal and impersonal 'concert' of Europe. The standard account insists on presenting the Final Act of the Congress of Vienna as an outcome of discrete and calculated exchanges between distinct international actors – be they the great powers or their diplomatic representatives. The claim here is that the standard IR account obscures the figurational embeddedness of international actors in the everyday processes and practices of diplomatic interactions. The first part of Chapter 1 details the standard IR narrative of the Congress of Vienna by focusing on the four key elements of its plot: (1) first, that it maintained peace on the continent from 1815 to 1914; (2) second, that it instituted a 'community of reason'; (3) third, that it was made possible because of the crucial role played by 'statesmen'; and (4) fourth, that it ushered in a European political community. It then briefly discusses the origins of this narrative in the post–World War II period and associates it with the work of Henry Kissinger.

Then, the second part of Chapter 1 sketches the outlines of alternative readings of the Vienna settlement. The argument is that the Concert system is best understood as shorthand for the connectivity and mutuality that emerged among those *who danced at Vienna* during the nine months of the Congress – *a community of dancing practice*. In other words, what the standard IR narrative calls *the Concert of Europe* is a reflection (if not a distant shadow) of *the waltzing movements that engaged those present at Vienna in the practices of collaborative diplomatic dancing.* As will become apparent, it was the waltzing that shifted strategic attitudes and enabled interpersonal relationships to flourish. The figurations of such dancing relationality assisted the moderation of differences in regime type and, gradually, began to be replaced by interpersonal connections (embedded in the very community and experience of such waltzing). What mattered in this setting were the roles engendered by the interactions at Vienna and which the participants played in the context of their interactions. Chapter 1 therefore recalls the relationality – and, in particular, the social practices, reciprocal figurations, and personal interconnections – which have been (seemingly carefully) excluded from the standard narrative. To the extent that it functioned, the Concert system was a contingent social practice made possible by fluid iterations of social transactions that percolated and gained salience in the context of ongoing and multiple relations during the nine months of the Congress.

This relational account of the Congress of Vienna should not be misunderstood as offering a better story – especially, not a normatively better one (not least because the relationality of this account is just as Eurocentric – even if more gender balanced – as the standard IR narrative). It merely provides a story (or rather an intersection of stories) which has been silenced for far too long. Although one does not have to venture far in order to uncover alternatives to the standard IR account of the Congress system, the attention is to the relationality of the interactions at Vienna. Just like the Viennese waltz, whose movements are always already different, global life not only moves in mysterious ways, but in the process it transforms, changes, and adapts in ways that cannot be anticipated in advance (and whose very patterns and practices adjust and change continuously and unexpectedly).

Chapter 2 then reviews two of the most prominent conversations on relationality in IR – those in its Anglophone and Sinophone variants. It needs to be stressed that these conversations are still very much taking place within each of these linguistic traditions individually, and there is not much in the way of dialogue between them. Yet before elaborating on the two kinds of relational turns in IR, the point of departure for such investigation is the recognition that IR is marked by a poignant lack of ontological pluralism. Regardless of their cultural commitments and linguistic mediums, the proponents of relationality agree that the IR mainstream is dominated by a substantialist vision of the 'world out there' as a closed system populated by states whose interactions are motivated by power-maximization in the pursuit of their own self-interests (Kavalski 2012). Thus, given the dynamics of linear causality that backstop this metanarrative, what comes to pass in world affairs is positioned as subject to anticipation as a result of reductionist models which postulate that all physical phenomena change in a gradual manner and following foreseeable trajectories. This 'atomistic ontology' asserts that all social phenomena are quantifiable and predictable (Kurki 2008: 107). The normative fundamentalism of this stance leads IR to adapt a mind-set of continuities that makes it difficult to address chance, change, and uncertainty (Whitman 2005: 119). In particular, the framework of instrumental-rational action has become the standard against which alternative claims are judged. Thus, the 'international' produced in this manner is an artefact of ontological and historical constructs with significant epistemic and ethical effects.

It is this context that provides the background for the parallel assessment of the Anglophone and Sinophone traditions of relationality. The first part of Chapter 1 details the conversation in the Anglophone literature. The focus here is on the processual relationalism of Patrick Thaddeus Jackson and Daniel H. Nexon and on the relational coexistence of Louiza Odysseos. Then, the second part of the chapter outlines the Sinophone accounts of relationality. The focus is on the relational theory of world affairs proposed by Qin Yaqing and the methodological relationalism of Zhao Tingyang. As is explained in Chapter 2, the selected representatives are neither the sole interlocutors, nor do they cover the full spectrum of relational perspectives either in the Anglophone or Sinophone strands of IR, let alone in the myriad other linguistic and cultural traditions of world affairs. Instead, the selected authors represent key nodes in the respective conversations on relationality. At the same time, the labels of Anglophone and Sinophone do not impute coherence among the interlocutors of relationality in either of these linguistic traditions. Rooted in the conviction that global life outlines a domain, space, narrative, and dynamic of 'multiple actors, traditions, and practices' (Katzenstein 2010: 23), the contributions to the relational turn in IR draw attention to the ongoing interpenetration between agency, structure, and order amongst the diversity of agency, form, and matter implicated in, enacting, and enabling global life. The insights from the conversations on relationality thus challenge the conviction that the appropriate way to acquire knowledge about the world is through the modelling of linear relationships with homogeneous independent variables that discern between discrete and stochastic and systemic effects (Earnest 2015; Rosenau 1990).

In this setting, Chapter 3 offers a dialogue between the Anglophone and Sinophone conversations on relationality. In particular, the chapter outlines how both the relational turn and IR theory would look if these were to be imagined with the help of the concept and practices of *guanxi*. As already indicated, this book deploys *guanxi* as a heuristic device that aids the hybridizing of the relational turns in IR. The chapter draws on the etymology of *guanxi* and brings into the IR conversation insights from an expansive literature on the relationality of *guanxi* from the fields of sociology, communication studies, and psychology. In particular, the contention of Chapter 3 is that the dynamic multiplicity of interdependent conditioning factors engenders an interpersonal realm whose complexity is only partially known to the participating actors. This outlook calls for a contextual attention to the transient constellations of factors and actors that affect the content, trajectories, and possible transformations in any social relationship – regardless of whether they occur on an interpersonal, regional, or global level. The underlying aim is to aid the ability to engage an ever-changing world.

In particular, the long-term orientation of *guanxi* inserts a modicum of predictability by lowering the transaction costs and ensuring the peaceful resolution of conflicts. At the same time, the decentring implicit in such an engagement draws attention to the idiosyncratic structural conditions and unique cultural categories that contribute to the participants' thinking about and involvement in interpersonal situations (Hwang 1987: 946). The claim then is that the encounter with the notion of *guanxi* evinces relational IR theorizing as an optics which both acknowledges the agency of 'others' and through which meanings are generated contingently through interactions in communities of practice, whose relations are premised on the variable reputations of participants and the necessity for ongoing reiteration of the commitment to do things together. This then backstops the attempt to outline a relational theory of IR beyond the Eurocentric frame.

The concluding chapter of the book therefore evokes the registers of worlding mutuality by elaborating the ways in which *guanxi* can help transcend the Eurocentric instrumentalism of disciplinary inquiry. In many ways, the very claim that the world is populated by and emerges through the continuous interactions between plentiful varieties of life and matter calls for the positing of alternative ontologies of IR. Thus, by demonstrating the 'radical interdependence', mutual co-constitution, and embeddedness of a multiplicity of figurations of relations, the interlocutors of the relational dialogues in IR seek to disrupt the linear reductionism of IR's ontological purview. The 'problem-solving' impulse backstopping the Eurocentric predilections of IR reveals a certain degree of wishful thinking in the disciplinary mainstream that global issues are not only 'amenable to the identification of a clear linear causation', but also that what matters in the study of world politics are phenomena that can be observed through such a 'deterministic mode of efficient linear inquiry' (Kavalski et al. 2018).

In the words of an intellectual fellow traveller: 'Realpolitik, geared toward extreme maximization of self-interest, disrupts long-term relational stability. *Relational-politik*, as an ethically more defensible alternative may lead international relations toward a more cooperative and harmonious direction' (Zhang 2015: 182; emphasis in original). The proposition is that the relationality outlined in this book engenders a rather gimballed view of global life. Just like a ship's compass – or a gimbal – the patterns of world affairs are made up of multiple, interdependent, and constantly shifting spheres of relations. The encounter with the gimbal of global life thereby acts as a reminder that knowledge (not just IR knowledge) is acquired and mediated relationally through diverse sets of practices. The ethical verso of such relationality is about the cultivation of attentiveness to the emergent, self-organizing, and contingent reality of global life. The ethical move is then to engage with the possibilities attendant in the living in an abundant, yet profoundly entangled world. At the same time, the proposition is that by removing the veil of the atomistic substantialist ontology of separation dominating the purview of IR, the endeavours of relationality reveal the impossibility of considering issues of ethics, ontology, epistemology, and politics in separation and as if they are not mutually implicated in one another (Kavalski et al. 2018). Redolent of the practices of *guanxi*, such a gimballed outlook implies that things in global life are not merely interconnected, but that they gain meaning and significance within complex webs of entanglements and encounters with others.

Notes

1 The meaning of the phrase 'relational turn' is explained in Chapter 2.

2 In her *Ordering International Politics*, Janice Bially-Mattern (2005: 5) explains 'uncovery' as a process that brings together the *discovery* of previously untouched perspectives and the *excavation* of insights from underneath layers of ossified or never-problematized knowledge.

3 The framework of itinerant translation is strongly influenced by the suggestion of IR as 'ecological narrative' developed by Krippendorf (2000).

4 In this setting Qin Yaqing has argued that 'relationality represents [a] natural way of life and as such reinforces their practice through the production of representational knowledge' (Qin 2017: 9).

5 The intention here is to make an analytical contribution to the understanding and explanation of the post-Western flavours of relationality in IR rather than illustrate how China has been able to gain a tremendous amount of goodwill and political capital in the Global South.

6 Such frustration has urged many to advocate for a creative implosion of the disciplinary mainstream: 'To decolonize IR is to *deschool* oneself from the discipline in its current dominant manifestations: to remember international relations, one needs to forget IR' (Krishna 2001: 407; emphasis added).

7 Jeanne Morefield (2014) suggests that mainstream IR scholarship is premised on the ongoing 'deflection' of attention from its illiberal outlook and racialized paradigms, as well as its systematic 'deflection' of responsibility for the imperial violence that it still backstops. The discussion of the concept of *guanxi* independent of the foreign policies and practices of the current Chinese government should not be misunderstood as an exercise of deflection. As will be explained shortly, *guanxi* is a characteristic of the 'Sinophonic world' as a whole, not just mainland China.

1 A relational dance or a scripted Concert of Europe?

Introduction

Was IR relational before the 'relational turn' that emerged in the late 1990s? How has such lack of relationality been institutionalized in the narratives and practices of IR? These are queries that most interlocutors of the relational turn – both in its Anglophone and Sinophonic variants – tend to obviate. Although there is no single event or account on which to pivot the development of the Columbus syndrome by the dominant perspectives on IR, the claim here is that the *unrelational* outlook can be traced back to the narrativization of the Congress of Vienna in IR (especially in the post–World War II period). The Vienna settlement is thus perceived to spawn a Concert of Europe, which maintained peace on the continent for the better part of the nineteenth century. At the same time, as a result of the arrangements at the Congress, the European system of international relations became a global one and relegated the rest of the world to a subjugated position. Thus, the usual image associated with the Vienna proceedings is that of statesmen sitting around tables and negotiating a framework for the post-Napoleonic order of Europe.

Yet what this account often overlooks is that the Congress did not take place over several days, nor even several weeks. It took the diplomatic representatives of European countries nine months to reach an agreement (which in the end seemed forced upon them by circumstances – namely, the return of Napoleon from exile). Thus, from November 1814 to June 1815, the participants at the Congress 'waltzed' and 'feasted' their way to an agreement on the post-Napoleonic international order. Both autobiographical accounts and news reports from the time demonstrate that it was the informality and the practice of daily interactions during these nine months that made possible the signing of the Final Act. For instance, in his memoirs, one of the participants at the concert, the French Count Auguste de La Garde-Chambonas, acknowledged that when he arrived at Vienna in September 1814, even though the Congress 'had been announced for several months, was not yet officially opened. The fêtes had, however, already commenced. In the abstract of the proceedings, it had been said that the conferences would be very short'. He went on to confess that:

The Congress had assumed the character of a grand fête in honour of the general pacification. Ostensibly it was a feast of rest after the storm, but, curiously enough, it offered a programme for life in its most varied movements. Doubtless, the foregathering of these sovereigns, ministers, and generals who for nearly a quarter of a century had been the actors in a grand drama supposed to have run its course, besides the pomp and circumstance of the unique scene itself, showed plainly enough that they were there to decide the destinies of nations. The mind dominated by the gravity of the questions at issue, could not altogether escape from the serious thoughts now and again obtruding themselves; but immediately afterwards the sounds of universal rejoicing brought a welcome diversion. Everyone was engrossed with pleasure. The love-passion also hovered over the assembly of kings, and had the effect of prolonging a state of abandonment and a neglect of affairs, both really inconceivable when taken in conjunction with upheavals the shock of which was still felt, and immediately before a thunderbolt which was soon to produce a singular awakening. The people themselves, apparently forgetting that when their rulers are at play, the subjects are doomed to pay in a short time the bills of such royal follies, seemed to be grateful for the foibles that drew their masters down to their level . . . It was, indeed, a picture which for many centuries will not be repeated.

(de La Garde-Chambonas 1902: 2–3 and 320)

It was in the context of such lavish celebrations that connections and mutuality began to emerge. In other words, the demise of the Concert system seems to reflect a breakdown in the 'waltzing' practices of relationality established at Vienna. However, rather than a complex and nuanced 'dance', IR narrates the experience of the Congress through the metaphor of a formal and impersonal 'concert' and, thus, expunging the 'dancing' relationality from the theoretical record. The standard account insists on presenting the Final Act of the Congress of Vienna as an outcome of discrete and calculated exchanges between distinct international actors – be they the great powers or their diplomatic representatives. Such imagination is framed by the perception of international life as a closed system of discrete autonomous actors whose interactions are subject to plausible calculations and predictable behaviours. The first part of the chapter details the standard IR narrative of the Congress of Vienna by focusing on the four key elements of its plot: (1) first, that it maintained peace on the continent from 1815 to 1914; (2) second, that it instituted a 'community of reason'; (3) third, that it was made possible because of the crucial role played by 'statesmen'; and (4) fourth, that it ushered in a European political community. It then briefly discusses the origins of this narrative in the post–World War II period and associates it with the work of Henry Kissinger.

The claim here is that the standard IR account obscures the figurational embeddedness of international actors in the quotidian processes and practices of diplomatic interactions. The second part of the chapter therefore sketches the outlines of alternative readings of the Vienna settlement. By drawing attention to the interactions occurring in what Metternich referred to as the 'singular intimacy' of ballrooms (quoted in Sluga 2014: 38), this chapter argues that the Concert system is best understood as shorthand for the connectivity and mutuality that emerged among those *who danced at Vienna* during the nine months of the Congress – *a community of dancing practice*. In other words, what the standard IR narrative calls *the Concert of Europe* is a reflection (if not a distant shadow) of *the waltzing movements that engaged those present at Vienna in the practices of collaborative diplomatic dancing*. As will become apparent, it was the waltzing that shifted strategic attitudes and enabled interpersonal relationships to flourish. The figurations of such dancing relationality assisted the moderation of differences in regime type and gradually began to be replaced interpersonal connections embedded in the very community and experience of such waltzing.

In particular, it was the very context of ballrooms and twirling movements that engendered a recognition that the world stage – just like the dance floor – is made up of multiple actors, each of them participating, shaping, and being shaped by the movements of international affairs (Ramel 2014: 140). At Vienna, each participant performed multiple roles, scripted by the various diplomatic dances in which they found themselves entangled. The waltz prompted movements and relations, which framed the diplomatic interactions of the Congress. Thus, and borrowing from a different context, the dancing relationality of the Concert system can be read as an aspect of transactional coalition building that produces a 'constituted outcome belonging in the realm of relations' and leads to 'new, visible and direct coordination of claims between two or more previously distinct actors' (Alimi et al. 2015: 26). This chapter therefore recalls the relationality – and, in particular, the social practices, reciprocal figurations, and personal interconnections – which have been (seemingly carefully) excluded from the standard narrative. To the extent that it functioned, the Concert system was a contingent social practice made possible by fluid iterations of social transactions that percolated and gained salience in the context of ongoing and multiple relations during the nine months of the Congress. The individual diplomats (and the states that they represented) are thus 'inseparable from the transactional contexts within which they are embedded' (Emirbayer 1997: 287–289). What mattered in this setting were the roles engendered by the interactions at Vienna and which the participants played in the context of their interactions. The Concert system was thereby (and ultimately) undone by the breakdown of this waltzing relationality. In particular, as the diplomats who had danced at Vienna were gradually replaced in the diplomatic corps of their respective countries, the community of dancing practice brought about *by* and *at* the Congress began to dissolve.

The narrative of the Concert of Vienna and its origins

Few events have captured the imagination of IR in the way that the Congress of Vienna has done. Many commentators have pointed out that together with the 1648 Peace of Westphalia, the Vienna settlement represents the most important milestone in the history of world politics (Albert 2016; Guo 2008; Pillalamarri 2016; Weitz 2008). In fact, some IR scholars ascertain that it was the Congress of Vienna that formally established the Westphalian system of territorial sovereignty and state-centric international relations (Mitzen 2005: 408; Reus-Smit 1999: 94; Teschke 2003: 5). In this respect, the Concert of Europe which was promulgated at the Congress of Vienna has become one of the defining narratives of the study and practice of IR. According to this storyline, the framework of the post-Napoleonic European order provides a unique – in fact, an extraordinary – mechanism for the regulation of inter-state rivalry and the institutionalization of cooperation.

The usually dry and uninspired language of IR grows surprisingly ebullient when it comes to the depiction of the Vienna system. For instance, the Concert of Europe is often referred to as a 'golden age' for diplomacy (Morgenthau 1958: 191) as well as peace and cooperation (Lauren 1983: 33). Some commentators have even censured 'historians' for assigning the Congress of Vienna 'a normal place in the series of international settlements, all of which are supposed to have worked for a time because of war weariness and temporary ideological solidarity'; and thus failing or refusing 'to recognize the truly revolutionary character' of the Vienna settlement, especially 'its uniqueness among all the peace settlements of European history':

> 1815 is the one and only time in European history when statesmen sat down to construct a peaceful international system and succeeded . . . This astonishing accomplishment in international politics, moreover, this uniquely non-utopian revolution, made possible much of the structural change and progress in nineteenth-century European society. *It is high time that this extraordinary accomplishment*

be squarely recognized, high time that an answer be given those who insist that international politics never really changes, that it always must remain in the old cycles of balance of power and systemic breakdown and conflict, high time to point to the Vienna era and say with Galileo, 'Eppur, si muove' (and yet, it moves).

(Schroeder 1992: 705; emphasis added)

Not surprisingly, therefore, both in the wake of World War II and the Cold War, as well as now with the growing realization of the significance of non-Western international actors on the world stage, scholars, policy-makers, and pundits have looked to the Concert of Europe as a model for managing the contingencies of a turbulent and complex global life.[1] Normatively speaking, what such accounts seem to find appealing is the promise that 'in global governance, good outcomes are possible without good intentions' (Mitzen 2013: 57). The following sections outline the main elements of the IR narrative of the Concert of Europe. The emphasis is on the substantialist imaginary that informs the standard account of the Vienna system.

The standard account of the Concert of Europe

Even a fleeting glance through any IR textbook would illustrate the nearly universal subscription to the narrative that the Congress of Vienna established peace and maintained order in the international system, which 'lasted until the First World War' and '*unquestionably* marked a shift away from the free-for-all and highly decentralized system of eighteenth-century international society towards a more managed hierarchical system' (Armstrong 2011: 44; emphasis added). The only moot point about this narrative seems to be the rationale behind the emergence of the Concert. Depending on their points of departure, different commentators have explained the nineteenth-century Vienna system as a result of the balance of power, as an outcome of institution building, as evidence of a security regime, as a product of ideational change, or some other reasoning. Yet regardless of the distinct points of departure for each of these justifications, all of them backstop a shared account about the outcome of the Congress of Vienna – namely, the emergence of a 'concert' system of harmonious international affairs. Thus, rather than reiterate different versions of the IR story of Concert of Europe, the following sections outline the main elements of its plot: (1) first, that it maintained peace on the continent from 1815 to 1914; (2) second, that it instituted a 'community of reason'; (3) third that it was made possible because of the crucial role played by 'statesmen'; and (4) fourth, that it ushered in a European political community.

The long nineteenth century of peace

Probably the most conspicuous element of this story is that the Concert of Europe has ensured 'ninety-nine years of general peace in Europe' (Holsti 1992: 49; Gress 1998: 313). Legions of IR students have been (and continue to be) schooled in the uncritical acceptance of a tale that 'after the Congress of Vienna . . . Europe experienced its longest period of stability since the rise of the modern state system' (Viotti and Kauppi 2013: 74). Thus, the period from 1815 to 1914 is oftentimes referred to as 'the "long" nineteenth century of peace' (Lyon 1970: 15; Abbenhuis 2014: 2–3; Holdbraad 1970) – 'the longest period of peace Europe has known' (Moisi 2014), 'allowing two generations to live without wars' (Matzka 2015). The assertion that the Vienna system sets the standard for diplomacy capable of maintaining peaceful political coordination is usually premised on a juxtaposition with the patterns of relations that dominated both the preceding and the following centuries.

Neither the system of international interactions that emerged in the wake of the 1713 Treaty of Utrecht nor the one established by the 1919 Treaty of Versailles seems to come anywhere near the achievements of the Congress of Vienna. Therefore, the conflicts that came to define both the eighteenth and the twentieth centuries offer ample confirmation for the defective nature of the peace settlements at Utrecht and Versailles, respectively. In contrast to these treaties, the Final Act of Vienna signed on 9 June 1815 provides a settlement which has had 'a better record [at maintaining peace] than any international peace conference either before or since' (Gress 1998: 313). In this respect, the alleged singularity of its pattern of international relations has become the distinguishing feature of the Concert of Europe.

The reference to 'concert' in this setting merely comes to distinguish the Vienna settlement from the alleged predisposition of world affairs to favour 'the sources of international dissension and discord [which] generally seems to overbalance the forces of harmony' (Elrod 1976: 159). Thereby, the Concert of Europe represents 'an equilibrating mechanism' producing and maintaining a system of order in which conflicts are resolved without the need to recourse to violence (Mitzen 2005: 408). At the same time, it furnishes 'a method of conducting international relations' which ushers in 'a pragmatic procedure aspir[ing] to nothing more than the preservation of the treaties of 1815 and the peaceful solution of specifically European problems' (Hoffman 1941: 683–686).[2] It is in this setting that the standard narrative of the Concert of Europe positions peace not merely as 'a precarious and precious matter', but also as an extremely rare occurrence in the turbulent dynamics of international politics.

A community of great power reason

The framing of the Vienna system as an arrangement in which states set aside their short-term gains in order to cultivate peace and cooperation accentuates the second element of the IR narrative of the Concert of Europe – namely, that it instituted a post-Napoleonic 'community of reason' (Dunne 1959: 132). According to this account, the international community at the time was able to 'come to its senses' because of the way it responded to the question of how to accommodate the forces of change in world affairs, while maintaining peace and security. The answer provided at the Congress of Vienna was nothing short of revolutionary. The task of political coordination on the international stage was the sole prerogative of a select category of international actors – which were labelled at the time as the 'great powers'.

Prior to the Congress of Vienna, the concept of great powers, as well as the division of international actors into major and minor powers, was virtually non-existent in diplomatic parlance. On the one hand, the reference to 'concert' in this setting reflects an agreement to allow 'the great powers of the day to sanction necessary alterations of the existing order [which] provided the means of legitimizing change without endangering the general system' (Elrod 1976: 169). On the other hand, the 'concert' label illustrates the pursuit of a functional commitment to avoid war between the great powers (Elrod 1976: 164; Mitzen 2005: 414). On a practical level, the Concert of Europe instituted an exclusive community of great powers – Austria, Britain, France, Prussia, and Russia. Known as the Committee of Five during the Congress of Vienna, the Concert of Europe stands as a shorthand for the 'unusually high and self-conscious level of cooperation among the major European powers' (Jervis 1986: 59).[3]

In practice, the allocation of the status as great power acted as an indication of extraordinary ordering roles on the world stage associated with the socially constructed prerogative of 'special rights and obligations in international society' (Reus-Smit 1999: 109). According to the standard narrative, as a system of joint great-power management, the Concert of Europe reflects an unprecedented level of self-restraint and willingness to accommodate the perspectives of the other great powers.[4] In this respect, it is ascertained that the Concert of Europe had major independent effects on the international behaviour of great powers (Kagan 1997: 22). The glue of the Vienna system was not merely great power tutelage, but aversion to unilateral action by any one of the great powers as a result of their commitment to act 'in concert'. This is what sets the Vienna system apart as 'an audacious experiment in international cooperation' (Jarrett 2013: 205). Thus, the community of reason represented by the pentarchy of great powers was seen to infuse a sense of predictability in a complex and anarchical international system.

The conferencing statesmen of Vienna

The third element of the IR narrative of the Concert of Europe is that it was made possible by the unusual acumen and skill of the individuals negotiating the outlines of the post-Napoleonic international order at Vienna. As Kalevi Holsti put it, it was in the discussions between five men – 'Metternich, Talleyrand, Alexander, Stein, and Castlereagh' – that the Concert of Europe was born (Hoslti 1992: 52). The standard story claims that it is the singular ability of the diplomatic representatives of the great powers to forego their narrow national self-interest that backstopped the emergence of the Vienna system. Usually, commentators underscore the 'patience', 'self-restraint', and 'uncommon willingness to appreciate the need for peace' demonstrated by the diplomats of the great powers at Vienna (Chapman 2002; Elson Roessler and Miklos 2003; Mowat 1930; Nichols 1971; Taylor 1954). Consequently, the reference to 'concert' turns the spotlight on the diplomatic record of the Vienna system, according to which the representatives of the great powers are said to have performed 'numerous acts of almost heroic national self-abnegation' (Holsti 1992: 19).

The concert can then be read as shorthand for the capacity of elite diplomats to single-handedly craft a peaceful system of international relations. According to this narrative, the Congress of Vienna emerges as one of these rare instances when 'history reveals that statesmen were more successful in some periods in the past than during others in managing and constraining unavoidable tensions' by compelling them 'to refrain from adventurous and aggressive foreign policies' (Elrod 1976: 159). The emphasis is on the 'conference diplomacy' pioneered at the Congress of Vienna, whose unique face-to-face interactions provided the glue keeping the Concert of Europe together. Such conference diplomacy allowed unprecedented opportunities for dialogue and deliberation. At the same time, it established 'a new inter-sovereign visibility' – that is, 'sovereigns who were accustomed to making foreign policy unilaterally found themselves justifying their policies to fellow sovereigns' (Mitzen 2005: 414). As a result, 'the policies of each were subject to the scrutiny and sanction of all' (Kagan 1997: 19).

The institutionalization of regularized meetings between the representatives of the great powers motivated by a shared commitment to the peaceful resolution of international crises has been labelled as nothing short of a 'revolution in diplomatic history' (Schenk 1947: 27). Such encounters allowed opportunities for 'habitual, confidential, and free intercourse between the Ministers of the Great Powers *as a body*' in the expectation that 'many pretensions might be modified, asperities removed, and causes of irritation anticipated and met' (Jarrett 2013: 205; emphasis added). Confirming the interpersonal camaraderie of these meetings, Lord Castlereagh, the British representative at the Congress of Vienna, referred to these face-to-face interactions with his European counterparts as 'reunions' (quoted in Webster 1934: 144). As the IR narrative of the Concert of Europe insists, such diplomatic 'reunions' for the representatives of the great powers furnished a socializing environment which made it possible for each of them to be 'persuaded in a friendly fashion' to comply with the rules and expectations of the Vienna system (Schroeder 1983: 7–9).

Establishing a European community

The final element of the IR narrative of the Vienna settlement is that it illustrated the establishment of the first ever European political community. The reference to 'concert' in this setting refers to the creation of a 'comprehensive political system' for the governance of the globe, which was rooted in and represented 'a type of politics of Europe in its entirety [gesamteuropäische Politik]' (Albert 2016: 103). In this reading, the Congress of Vienna promulgated a functioning system of European governance (Holdbraad 1970 and 1971; Schroeder 1994; Slantchev 2005). What made the Vienna system work therefore was that the great powers of the day recognized both their shared European identity and responsibility for European affairs. In this respect, even if not yet a 'community of destiny', the Congress seems to have forged a European community of shared interests and commitments.

The instrumental aim of the Congress was to develop 'European solutions to European problems' (Elrod 1976: 162). In other words, 'the task of the men at Vienna was indeed to write what seemed to amount to a general European institution' (Hoffman 1941: 683). In this respect, the Final Act of the Congress of Vienna provided not only a framework for 'multilateral stewardship' of European affairs, but also an agreement that any treaties emerging from this and other future such meetings would be treated as the ' "law of Europe" binding on all states' (Holsti 1992: 39). In this respect, Friedrich von Gentz, the secretary to the Congress and Metternich's advisor, described the Vienna settlement as,

> uniting the sum total of states in a federation under the direction of the major powers . . . The second-, third-, and fourth-rate sates submit in silence and without any previous stipulation to the decisions jointly taken by the preponderant powers; and *Europe seems to form finally a great political family under the auspices of an areopagus of its own creation.*
>
> (quoted in Morgenthau 1948: 436–437; emphasis added)

At the same time, even though the decisions were taken only by the great powers, due to bandwagonning and alliance building of the smaller countries, 'all European countries' felt like they had a stake in the Concert (Soutou 2000: 131). In particular, the contention is that by preventing the transformation of the Holy Alliance into an instrument for the effective governance of Christendom, the Congress of Vienna appears to have secured 'the triumph of a principle that was strictly *European* and based on a recognition of the pluralism of Europe's political constitution' (Hoffman 1941: 685; emphasis added). It was thus in the discussions at the Congress that the 'idea of Europe' superseded the notion of 'universal Christendom'; although this was a process that had already been set into motion with the Treaties of Westphalia, Vienna formalized that the ' "whole" in whose name all diplomacy was aimed' was the European system 'whose stability was secured through mutual toleration' (Mitzen 2005: 408; Satow 1925: 297). In this respect, the Congress of Vienna becomes an occasion for the (re)birth of the 'idea of Europe' as a 'unique community of reason' whose political consciousness was savaged by the experience of the Napoleonic Wars and draws on the attenuated awareness as well as memory of 'the lost unity of the past' (Dunne 1959: 132).[5]

The thrust of this narrative is that the exercise of power by the Concert allowed the great powers to maintain authority without humiliating secondary states. The Concert system thus furnished a normative basis for the appropriate conduct of European affairs. As a result, most likely unwittingly, the Congress of Vienna grew to be perceived both as 'a deliberative assembly of Europe' and as an indication that Europe can be treated as 'a constitutional whole' (Peterson 1945: 535). The Concert system thus evidences a rationalization of 'the medieval notion of Europe as Christendom into the notion of Europe as a balance-of-power system' (Mitzen 2005: 410). At the same time, at least discursively, 'the European states system was treated as a kind of imaginary super-actor with the same aspirations as the individual actors that made it up' (Osiander 1994: 111). It was thus the social bonds and practices among those present in Vienna that helped nurture a sense of shared Europeanness among them.

Origins of the standard (unrelational) account of the Concert of Europe

The fairly uniform narrative of the Concert of Europe, as well as the general agreement on the key elements of its story, bespeaks a fairly high degree of standardization. How and when did such standardization occur? Is there a particular period or an individual setting this process into motion? In response to these queries, this section suggests that there appears to have been a coalescence of perspectives in the aftermath of World War II, not least because of the efforts of Henry Kissinger. Such a claim should not be misunderstood as a suggestion either that Kissinger is the sole author of the narrative of the Concert of Europe or that there weren't any earlier instances of this story. Instead, the point here is that it was the inception of the Cold War which prodded many commenters to revisit the arrangements of the Vienna system. Due to his standing in between academe and policy making, Kissinger was uniquely positioned to champion the consolidation of a particular reading of the Concert of Europe.

It is certainly not a coincidence that the account of the Vienna system which became dominant in IR was the one favoured by Kissinger:

> It may not have fulfilled all the hopes of an idealistic generation, but it gave this generation something perhaps more precious: a period of stability which permitted their hopes to be realized without a major war or a permanent revolution.
>
> (Kissinger 1957: 5)

Although the lack of relationality seems to have been part and parcel of IR discourses since the mythologization of the origins of Westphalian sovereignty (Teschke 2003), the formalization of substantialism in IR's outlook can be traced back to the narrativization of the Congress of Vienna in the theory and practice of world affairs. The Concert system upholds the assumption of a 'world of atomized self-seeking egotistic individuals', which sets in motion claims that international organizations 'derive from voluntary agreements among juridically equal actors' (Krasner 1983: 6–11). Perhaps unsurprisingly, Henry Kissinger's doctoral dissertation on the topic offers one of the best illustrations of the IR myths about the Concert of Europe. As he notes, 'the Congress [of Vienna] was expected to have a primarily symbolic significance'. Its momentous effects were merely 'accidental', because an

> international order is rarely born out of *the consciousness of harmony*. For even when there is an agreement about legitimacy, the conceptions of the requirements of security will differ with the geographical position and the history of the contending powers. Out of just such a conflict over the nature of the equilibrium, the Congress of Vienna fashioned a settlement which lasted for almost exactly a century.
>
> (Kissinger 1957: 143–147; emphasis added)

What Kissinger is saying here is that peace is rarely an option for world politics because international life is unrelational (or, to use his words, it lacks a 'consciousness of harmony'). Yet what made possible the so-called 'Hundred Years' Peace' (a period in European affairs stretching from the

end of the Napoleonic Wars to the outbreak of World War I) was not relationality, but the acumen of diplomats well versed in the principles of the
balance of power: for Kissinger, balance of power represents

> the classic expression of the lesson of history that no order is safe
> without physical safeguards against aggression. Thus, [the Congress
> of Vienna] created a balance of forces which, because it conferred a
> relative security, came to be generally accepted, and whose relation-
> ships grew increasingly spontaneous as its legitimacy came to be taken
> for granted.
>
> (Kissinger 1957: 318)

According to Kissinger, such statesmanship was rooted in a Machiavellian
belief in 'the ruler's ability (or lack of it) to react to incentives or disincen-
tives in an appropriate manner' (Cesa 2014: 20). In his own elaborations,
Kissinger admits that 'it is fortunate for the lessons posterity may draw from
this period that the chief protagonists were men of marked individuality'
(Kissinger 1957: 316). In this respect, for Kissinger international order was
not about fairness, but about the acceptance of (or an agreement about) its
arrangements by the main actors of the day (that is, by the great powers). In
practice, this meant that

> Every statesman must attempt to reconcile what is considered just
> with what is considered possible. What is considered just depends
> on the domestic structure of his state; what is possible depends on its
> resources, geographic position and determination, and on the resources,
> determination and domestic structure of other states.
>
> (Kissinger 1957: 5)

True statesmanship, as the Congress reveals, is located at the cusp 'between
the effort to escape time and the need to survive in it':

> It is the inextricable element of history, this conflict between inspiration
> and organization. Inspiration implies the identification of the self with
> the meaning of events. Organization requires discipline, the submission
> of the will of the group. Inspiration is timeless; its validity is inherent
> in its conception. Organization is historical, depending on the material
> available at the given period. Inspiration is a call for greatness; organi-
> zation is a recognition that mediocrity is the usual pattern of leader-
> ship. To be effective politically, one requires organization . . . [T]he
> statesman strives to keep latent the tension between organization and
> inspiration; to create a pattern of obligations sufficiently spontaneous

to reduce to a minimum the necessity for the application of force, but, at the same time, of sufficient firmness not to require the legitimization of a moment of exaltation.

(Kissinger 1957: 317)

For Kissinger, therefore, this revisionist story had particular appeal, as it held the potential to dispel the nuclear nightmares unleashed by the nascent Cold War of his day – the key seemed to be statesmen willing to accept the inviolability of each other's spheres of influence (and thereby unable to imagine any other interaction on the world stage). As others have already pointed out, for Kissinger, the Congress of Vienna epitomized both (1) 'a lesson of enduring value for his adoptive country. What long-dead European aristocrats like Metternich and Castlereagh could teach the United States was how to constrain a revolutionary superpower – for France read the USSR – and bind it into the rules of the international game' (Mazower 2013: 3); and (2) hope for softening 'the stark confrontation of the Cold War by building a multipolar system comparable with the old Concert of Europe, in which the world would be governed by a consortium of the United States, the Soviet Union, Japan, and Europe' (Howard 2000: 83–84). For Kissinger, his story of the Congress of Vienna narrates a way both of coming to terms with and making governable (i.e. subject to control) what he perceived as the coming disorder of the Cold War. The vision of great powers balancing their interests at diplomatic roundtables drove promises of security (which were much preferable to the nightmarish 'state of nature' of nuclear war). Kissinger insisted that, all other things being equal, order can be constructed in discrete bargaining contexts as a result of series of optimizing negotiations by autonomous and rational international actors. Thus, the Concert system provides a convincing historical source of probabilistic and law-like regularities that can be utilized for the explanation and understanding of other similar phenomena (Alimi et al. 2015: 33). At the same time, such narrative is the outcome of a deliberately pursued vision in which antagonism and anarchy are positioned as bearing the required checks and balances for ensuring the mutual limits and sovereignty of states (Cudworth et al. 2018).

The dance of Vienna and the elision of relationality

The discussion in the preceding section should have made apparent how well ensconced in the literature on IR is the narrative of the Congress of Vienna as a unique moment in the development of world affairs. Not only did it provide a framework that kept peace in Europe for nearly a century, but the Concert system that it promulgated advances a paragon for the management of any conflict. The moral of the accepted story of the Congress of Vienna is that all it takes to resolve international disagreements peacefully is statesmen capable of rational discussion and great powers willing to pursue their self-interest through calculated and dispassionate balancing. Such account is conspicuously substantialist and prioritizes the actors involved at the expense of the relations and processes that made possible the Vienna settlement. The aim here is not merely to critique the existing account of the Congress of Vienna in IR, but to demonstrate that it has institutionalized a substantialist reading not only of the Concert of Europe, but IR more broadly.

The standard IR account rests on a decontextualized analysis which focuses selectively on some of the activities of the representatives of the five great powers. Consequently, the standard account presents an ordering principle which not merely denies alternative narrativizations, but also legitimizes a particular modality for the explanation and understanding both of the Congress of Vienna and IR. A good case in point here is the particularly scathing review by the historian George Strong (1987) of Susan Mary Alsop's monograph, *The Congress Dances*. Strong finds it intolerable that Alsop's account dares to depart from the accepted narrative of the Congress of Vienna. As he noted,

> But other than giving a lively description of events leading up to certain selected nocturnal activities of members of the great world, Alsop focuses on *none of the great political events that took place during this period*... Indeed, if there is a focus in this reading, it is on the great romp.
> (Strong 1987: 103; emphasis added)

While confirming the entrenchment of the standard narrative of the Congress of Vienna, Strong's critique also suggests that dissident voices are permitted only to the extent that they do not challenge the authorized imagination of the 'great political events that took place during this period'. As he goes on to acknowledge (seemingly unaware of the intellectual heritage of his assumptions):

> After all, one can hardly have expected dashing, brave diplomats to have been all work and no play. Of course, the handsome young men are seeking love, and the women are of easy virtue. And so it was that the sexes came together very often. Nevertheless, beyond the sheets of the boudoir, one learns very little of what made the congress dance when its members faced one another over green baize tables.
> (Strong 1987: 103)

Such assertion offers a nearly perfect narrative reproduction of Jean-Baptiste Isabey's drawing of the 'concert diplomacy' established at Vienna – a gathering of resolute men in the stately rooms of the Geheime Hof und Staatskanzlei (now the Austrian Federal Chancellery). Yet both Strong's account and Isabey's depiction omit that during the nine months of the Congress of Vienna, the Committee of Five met only 41 times, most of these meetings lasted for less than an hour, and their discussions focused on procedure (especially the agenda for the next meeting) rather than actual negotiations of the European post-Napoleonic order. Instead 'the real business' of the Congress was carried out informally (Peterson 1945: 539). Some have even suggested that France's inclusion within the great powers was due to Talleyrand's 'culinary diplomacy' rather than his negotiating skills. For instance, a major 'conflict' erupted between the representatives of various European nations: which one is home to the best cheese. Talleyrand proposed that the issue should be solved through a contest, which he organized. Sixty cheeses were entered in the competition, and the ultimate winner ('*le roi des fromages*') was the French 'Brie de Meaux' – thus solidifying France's reinstatement among the 'big cheeses' of European affairs.[6] Staying with the culinary theme, it was the Congress of Vienna that popularized Viennese cuisine (Wiener Küche) as a unique mélange of Czech, Hungarian, and Italian cooking traditions which coexisted and complemented each other (Charles and Carl 2014: 55–57). In this respect, it was the very hybridity and intermixing of ingredients and dishes that illustrate the type of relationality that marked the interactions at the Congress.

In this respect, the bulk of the interactions was informal and took place not in conference rooms, but in the salons, dancing halls, cafes, and boudoirs of Vienna. The standard IR narrative of the Congress of Vienna overlooks the very relationality that made possible the signing of the Final Act – nine months of all kinds of intercourse and interaction in the environs of Vienna between the negotiating parties, allowing for diverse sets of connections to emerge. Thus, if one is to look beyond the standard IR narrative of the Congress – especially in the history of ideas, musicology, cultural and literary studies, philosophy, sociology, etc. – a far richer and vivid story emerges. This alternative account takes place in Viennese cafes, salons, and dancing halls animated by waltzing figures and vibrant music. Brimming with relationality, this story invokes the metaphor of 'dance' – as opposed to the 'concert' – to illuminate the multiplicity of social interactions between men and women heralding not just from the five great powers, but from all the European countries at the time. This relational account of the Congress of Vienna should not be misunderstood as offering a better story – especially not a normatively better one (not least because the relationality of this account is just as Eurocentric – even if more gender balanced – as the standard IR narrative). It merely provides a story (or rather an intersection of stories) which has been silenced for far too long. Although one does not have to venture far in order to uncover alternatives to the standard IR account of the Congress system, the attention is on the relationality of the interactions at Vienna. The following sections challenge the key elements of the accepted narrative of the Concert of Europe.

Peace!? What peace?

Perhaps the key element of the standard IR narrative about the Congress of Vienna, the assertion that it provided a governance mechanism able to maintain peace on the continent for nearly a century, is surprisingly easy to dispute. To begin with, there are quite a few commentators who renounce the very peace-keeping function of the Vienna system. As some have argued, 'it was the peace which maintained the Concert and not the Concert that maintained the peace' (Medlicott 1956: 18; Elrod 1976: 160; Gulick 1955: 156–159). The point here is that the Concert had little (if any) substantive bearing on the behaviour of states – regardless of whether they were great powers or not. In fact, the claim is that if such peace-keeping function existed at all, it was never more than a 'simulacrum of stability' (Zamoyski 2001: 569) – that is, a rhetorical façade for the pursuit of more tangible and narrow self-interest (Rendall 2000). In fact, the phrase 'diplomatic theatre' has its origins in what many at the time (especially in the host country of Austria) considered to be a vacuous and pointless expense associated with the 'evacuation of purpose from the residual and retrograde diplomatic entertainments performed at the Congress of Vienna' (Welch 2017: 211). Even someone as invested in the success of the gathering as Friedrich von Gentz found himself conceding that:

> Never have the expectations of the general public been as excited as they were before the opening of this solemn assembly. People were confident of a general reform of the political system of Europe, of the Guarantee of eternal peace, even of the return of the Golden age. Yet, it produced only restitutions decided beforehand by the force of arms, arrangements between the great powers, unfavourable to the future balance and the maintenance of peace in Europe, and some quite arbitrary rearrangements on the possessions of the lesser states, but not one act of a more elevated character, not one measure of public order or security which might compensate humanity for any part of its long sufferings or reassure it as to the future.
>
> (quoted in Zamoyski 2001: 550)

In this respect, a number of commentators have asserted that the 'long nineteenth century' is marked by far more conflict and rivalry and far less cooperation than the standard account of the Concert of Europe would admit (Kagan 1997: 50; Richardson 1994). At the same time, while agreeing in principle with the peace-keeping function of the Congress of Vienna, others have disputed its longevity. Depending on their point of departure and framework of analysis, different authors point to different dates when the Concert system ceased to exist. These range from the 1822 Congress of Verona (Nichols 1971), through the death of the Russian Tsar Alexander I in 1825 (Setton-Watson 1955), the expulsion of France from the Concert in July 1840 (Bullen 1979), the revolutions that swept through the continent in 1848 (Kratochwil and Ruggie 1986), to the 1853–1856 Crimean War (Elrod 1976).

In other words, even if it did exist as a system for the maintenance of peace on the continent and the management of order between the great powers of the day, the Concert of Europe was hardly a century-long phenomenon. In particular, as the so-called 'Eastern question'[7] became the diplomatic flavour of the month, the cooperative aptitude of the great powers seemed to wane. Thus, although the Crimean War furnishes the most prominent indication of the collapse of the Vienna system, the divisions between the great powers were already becoming apparent with the outbreak of the Greek War of Independence (Elrod 1976; Slantchev 2005). According to these accounts, 'the culture of peace' associated with the Concert of Europe was not such a tangible commodity of European diplomatic interactions during the nineteenth century (Schultz 2007: 43).

A community of reason or a community of waltzing?

The second element of the standard account of the Vienna settlement is that the Congress system introduced a modicum of predictability in European affairs ushered in by the pentarchy of five great powers as the arbiters of international interactions. Such rationalization furnished a management mechanism trough balancing the interests of the most important continental actors. In this respect, the main connotation of the community of reason backstopping the Concert of Europe is diplomacy by conference/consultation (Elrod 1976: 162). Diplomats were therefore construed as ' "scientist[s]" of politics, coolly and unemotionally arranging [their] combinations in an age increasingly conducting policy "by causes" ' and free from any 'sentimental attachments' (Kissinger 1957: 319). Yet the occurrences at Vienna during the nine months of the Congress seem to presage a different kind of rationality – one whose movement and contingency seem to undermine the veracity of this proposition.

In fact, in contrast to the formal and impersonal diplomatic encounters depicted by the standard IR narrative of the Vienna settlement, the diplomatic interactions of the Congress were quite intimate and involved, what some of a more anthropological bent may call 'deep hanging out'.[8] The diplomatic representatives of European nations quite literally spent time together – in particular, in informal settings[9] – which led to the development of personal connections and entanglements. In fact, the diaries and reports from the time indicate that the notion of conference diplomacy was being defined in Vienna as a context for ongoing dances. As the aging Prince de Ligne quipped famously, 'the Congress dances, but does not move forward' (quoted in Schnitzler 1954: 103).

As many cultural commentators have pointed out, the origins of the myth of 'gay Vienna' are profoundly intertwined with the happenings at the Congress itself. In particular, it was during that gathering that the reputation of Vienna as a city of fun and entertainment captured global imaginations (Shorske 1961: 3). The cultural historian Henry Schnitzer (1954) observed that most contemporaries considered the gathering to be a disappointment. In the words of the Prussian Minister Freiherr von Stein, the 'deliberations' of the Congress were best characterized as 'distraction, lack of profundity or some, dullness and coldness of other, imbecility and vulgarity of still others, frivolity of all were the reasons were the reasons why *no great, noble, beneficial idea could be brought into being*' (quoted in Schnitzer 1954: 104; emphasis added). Another commentator noted that the exuberant 'social amenities' of the Congress, and especially 'their excessive accumulation', led to 'increased lethargy and diminished concentration' among the diplomatic representatives (quoted in Nicholson 1946: 159). One of the French emissaries noted that 'festivities followed one another without interruption; it seemed as if one considered every moment not dedicated to pleasure as lost' (quoted in Schnitzer 1954: 104). In short, the Congress represented 'the greatest party the world had ever seen' (Zamoyski 2001: 573).

In particular, the diplomatic parlaying of the conference could hardly be distinguished from the 'dancomania' that gripped the representatives of the European nations (Sluga 2015: 3). For instance, the Russian Tsar Alexander I

> danced for forty successive nights until he collapsed and became seriously ill from exhaustion. Lord Castlereagh, the British Minister, claimed that for him dancing was an essential relaxation . . . so essential, in fact, that when no ladies were available he grabbed the chairs of his lodging to whirl them around.
>
> (Schnitzer 1954: 104)

In fact, things became so heated at the New Year's ball organized at the residence of the Russian ambassador Prince Razumvsky that an accidental fire burned the whole palace to the ground (Jarrett 2013: 119). It is not surprising then that some Russian representatives declared waltz to be 'the mortal enemy' of the Congress (Vick 2014: 52). It seemed like the dancing would have never stopped were it not for Napoleon's return from exile; in fact, it is alleged that his first words upon setting foot on French soil are: 'Behold! The Congress is dissolved' (quoted in Murphy 1985: 80).

Such accounts reveal that rather than a calculating community of reason, the Concert system emerging from Vienna depended on the personal disposition and interpersonal connections of diplomats. Such dispositions were contingent on and formed in the context of specific interactions. As Metternich observed, it was the 'singular intimacy' of ballrooms that is 'without example in the annals of European history' and which allowed an agreement to be reached without the 'sending of [any] couriers, no written negotiations, no medium between the Courts' (quoted in Sluga 2014: 38–39). Another participant acknowledged that

> A kingdom was cut into bits or enlarged at a ball; an indemnity was granted in the course of a dinner, a constitution was planned during a hunt . . . Acrimonious discussions and 'dry-as-dust' statements were replaced for the time being, as if by magic, by the most polite forms in any and every transaction. *Negotiating as from brother to brother*, in a manner that would have rejoiced the heart of Catherine the Great, *the sovereigns quite amicably and without the least hurry arranged 'their little affairs'*; they gave one the impression of wishing to please the philosophic dream of Abbé Saint-Pierre.
>
> (de La Garde-Chambonas 1902: 1–3; emphasis added)

In this respect, it could be argued that the label of Concert of Europe refers to the connections that emerged among the diplomatic representatives *who danced at Vienna*. Thus, the assertions by contemporaries that the Concert system began to collapse in the early 1820s could be explained with the removal of some of those 'dancers' from the diplomatic corps of their countries. For instance, with the deaths of the Russian Tsar Alexander I and the British representative Lord Castlereagh, the community of dancers began to unravel, and with them the practices (and memories) that bound them together began to disappear. Metternich himself went as far as acknowledging the significance of this relationality when he admitted that Castlreagh's death was a great diplomatic 'misfortune': 'Castlereagh was the only man in his country who had learned to understand me. Now several years will have to elapse until somebody else acquires a similar degree of confidence' (quoted in Kissinger 1957: 312).

The waltzing movements and musical accompaniment to the diplomatic interactions at the Congress both shifted strategic attitudes and enabled interpersonal relationships to flourish. The informality, vim, and verve of the Viennese waltz infused a recognition that the world stage – just like the dance floor – is made up of multiple actors, each of them participating, shaping, and being shaped by the movements of international affairs (Ramel 2014: 140). It is in the figurations of such dancing relationality that differences in regime type began to lose their significance and instead interpersonal connections (rooted in the community of such dancing practices) began to shift and shape the dispositions of participating diplomats. Thus, in the words of Metternich, it was as a result of the informality of the ballroom that, '[t]he tongue is untied, the heart opens and the need to make oneself understood often takes over from the rules of cold and severe calculation' (quoted in Zamoyski 2001: 250)

And how about the women of Vienna?

A significant feature of the relationality that emerged at the Congress was the agency of women.[10] As one of the participants noted, 'Never did a city hold within its walls as many remarkable women as did the capital of Austria during the nine months of the Congress' (de La Garde-Chambonas 1902: 38). Although their roles in diplomacy were largely informal and associated with drawing rooms, ballrooms, and bedrooms, this did not prevent them (in fact some have argued that it actually enhanced) the opportunity to exert influence over the proceedings and, more broadly, European politics at the time. Yet female agency has been completely written off from the standard IR narrative about the Concert of Europe. As one historian of the Congress of Vienna acknowledged,

> never before – or after – have a group of statesmen and politicians, assembled solely and exclusively to deal with matters of commonweal interest, laboured so extensively and decisively under the influence of women – not in Munster, nor in Rastatt, not in Versailles, nor yet in San Francisco.
>
> (Spiel 1968: 6; see also Sluga 2015: 2)

As wives, mistresses, and hostesses, their involvement 'oiled the wheels' of diplomacy, turning European affairs into profoundly intimate and interpersonal 'social politics' (Chalus 2000: 669). In particular, the emergence of the salon as an idiosyncratic institution for gossip, networking, and news made diplomacy 'an area ideal for colonization by female politicians'

(Richardson 2013: 176). In fact, one commentator remarked, that 'no man could rise to prominence except against the background of a salon, and over every salon a woman ruled' (Cooper 2010: 18). In particular, salons provided unique fora for political negotiation, which not only coincided with, but also had direct bearing on the professionalization of European diplomacy (Mierhofer et al. 2008; Sluga and James 2015). The term 'salon diplomacy' provided thereby a shorthand for the relational nature of international interactions at the time (Enloe 1989: 96; Wieland 2012: 271–285).

In this setting, the Congress of Vienna became an important marker for the roles of women, as well as the ambivalence associated with their agency in the domain of international politics. A number of participants observed that it was 'the intrigues of women that influenced the politics of States' (quoted in Sluga 2015: 4). In particular, 'independent' women such as Princess Katherina Bagration, Wilhelmina Duchess of Sagan, and Princess Dorothea Lieven (among many others present in Vienna) contributed at least as much to the Final Act of Congress as the statesmen with whom they consorted (Charmley 2005; Cromwell 2007; Landes 2008; Sluga 2014). At the same time, as the feminist historiographer of the Congress, Glenda Sluga (2015) discerns, because the involvement of women in the proceedings was not part of the official record, their presence and agency have been expunged from history. Not only this, but their involvement had been actively opposed by some of the diplomatic representatives – for instance, Baron Rosenkrantz, the Danish Minster of Foreign Affairs, complained that the Congress was destined to be a failure because of 'the meddling of women' (quoted in Sluga 2015: 7). Not surprisingly, therefore, in the wake of the Congress, women were gradually excluded from diplomatic conferences. Writing only a couple of years later, in 1817, Frederick Lamb – a British diplomat – participating at a conference in Frankfurt on German unification, complained that in contrast to Vienna, 'the lack of women opening their homes had stymied negotiations' (quoted in Sluga 2015: 11).

Effecting a European community or European supremacy?

Although indeed a European political community might have emerged as a result of the waltzing during the Congress of Vienna, a central feature of that community was its shared commitment to ensuring European supremacy not only over European, but also global affairs. In other words, the atomistic lopsidedness of the standard narrative of the Concert of Europe overlooks the very condition of its possibility – the racism backstopping 'the idea of Europe' that emerged in Vienna. Indeed, if one concurs with the main claim of the Concert system that there has been no military conflict between the European great powers until the beginning of the twentieth century (with the obvious exception of the Crimean War, which was itself an unfortunate 'accident' according to this account), the post-1815 period marked one of the most violent stages in the systematic exploitation, theft, and genocide of various non-European peoples (Krishna 2001). In this respect, there is nothing accidental about the Hundred Years' Peace as Kissinger (and others) seem to impute. The Congress of Vienna reflected a conviction shared between the participating white, upper-class men and women that their Christian European ways were superior to those of the rest of the world (in fact, this conviction was instrumental to the relationality that emerged between them at Vienna).

It was the conviction of a shared European civilizational supremacy which provided a shared background of understanding among the diplomatic representatives of various European countries and assisted them in striking an agreement that there is not much to be gained from squabbling over supremacy in Europe – not least because there is so much land 'out there' still to be conquered. As Hans Morgenthau, one of the fathers of IR, rather bluntly acknowledged, a key contributing factor to 'the success of the Concert of Europe in preventing general wars' was the agreement that no great power would 'take up arms against another great power in order to expand into the *politically empty spaces* of Africa and Asia' (Morgenthau 1948: 369; emphasis added). The point here is that the standard IR narrative of the Congress of Vienna precipitates the lack of relational theorizing and practices sanctioned by IR. It is in this setting that one of the most enduring legacies of the unrelationality codified at the Congress of Vienna emerges – the wilful silencing of alternative worldviews through the legitimation of Western containment of the 'politically empty spaces' of the non-West. The point here is not merely that those hankering after the nearly half a century of peace of the Cold War perpetuate the same racialized amnesia underpinning Kissinger's yearning for the stability of the Concert of Europe – they close their eyes to the violence accompanying the 'proxy wars' inflicted by the two superpowers in the very spaces colonized during the Hundred Years' Peace. Instead, it is the denial of the possibility of a relational IR in the narrativization of the Concert of Europe that perpetuates the 'profound violence' against its non-Western counterparts, both by refusing to offer them a formal recognition 'for their critical role in *making* world politics' and by denying non-Western ways and forms of knowing '*epistemically*' (Ling 2015: 1; emphasis added). To put it bluntly, the values associated with and underpinning the standard IR narrative of the Vienna settlement are forged in the kiln of empire and exploitation.

In this respect, whereas the idea of the Concert might have been steeped in a tradition recognizing the pluralism of Europe, its framing was explicitly designed to deny it to the rest of the world. The choice that the Concert system seemed to offer was either 'the gradual reproduction of all parts of the world in the image of the West' or 'descent into irrationality' (Hutchings 2008: 156). Thus, the value rationality of the Vienna dance excluded non-European others 'more for what they are than what they have done' (Donnelly 2006: 147). Symbolically, this was demonstrated through the exclusion of the Ottoman Empire from the Congress (Adanir 2016: 20; Jarrett 2013: 69–157). Thus, when the Sublime Porte 'sent an emissary' to the Congress (even though it had not received an official invitation), the Ottoman representative was 'kept out' (Mitzen 2013: 95). Some might consider this snub a precursor to Turkey's later attempt to join another European community – that of the EU. In this respect, the Congress not only instituted a 'collective hegemony' of the great powers (Jarrett 2013: 180), it also provided the foundation for the 'legalized hegemony' (Simpson 2004: 68) of the West/Global North over the rest of the world. Thus, the exclusion of the Ottoman Empire inheres a logic of homogeneity backstopping the aggressive expansion of the European international society during the nineteenth century (Haukkala 2008: 39).[11]

Closer to the ambit of this book, the Vienna settlement continues to reverberate in China's strategic culture and commitment to national rejuvenation – a narrative that provides the discursive hub linking the domestic and international concerns of the country. To begin with, the suppression of the Boxer Rebellion (1898–1900) and the subsequent occupation of China evidence a key feature of the Concert system – European collaboration to quash resistance to colonialism through the institutionalization of violence, the subjugation of rival political centers of allegiance, and the assimilation (or outright genocidal purges) of cultures considered uncivilized (Cudworth et al. 2018). In this respect, China has self-consciously positioned its current rise to global prominence as a reaction to the memory and trauma of what it calls the 'Century of Humiliation' inflicted on the country by the Hundred Years' Peace. The clash of these two imaginaries contributes to the mixture of confidence and consternation with which the IR mainstream tries to make sense of Beijing's international outreach. As Adam Watson has acknowledged, European countries have tended to apply a 'standard of civilization' to their non-European counterparts, who are judged not merely 'by how they conducted their external relations, but also by how they governed themselves' (Watson 1987: 151). Quoting the Austrian foreign minister and host of the Congress, Klemens von Metternich, Watson suggests that the aim of the Vienna system is to protect 'the spiritual, religious, and social values of their common European civilization' (Watson 1985: 71–72). In other words, 'empire-building outside of Europe' (Dunne 1959: 144), more than anything else, backstopped the framing of the Concert system by diverting attention from all-out conflict on the continent. In short, the European

relationality begotten at the Congress constituted a Concert system delin-
eating a civilizational boundary, beyond whose demarcations lived forces
disruptive of and inferior to meaningful political life (and, thus, they had to
suffer 'the white man's burden') (Yurdusev 2003: 126–145).

Conclusion

The chapter has outlined two narratives of the Congress of Vienna. In the
first part, it details a story that is almost universally accepted by the IR mainstream. This story draws attention to the diplomatic interactions between
the statesmen representing the five great powers at the Congress. The claim
is that it was during the wheeling and dealing of these negotiations that a
Concert of Europe emerged, representing a system for the management of
European affairs that managed to maintain peace on the continent almost
until the outbreak of World War I. As it has been demonstrated, prodded by
his own concerns about the nascent Cold War confrontation between the
United States and the Soviet Union, Henry Kissinger was instrumental in
popularizing this story in the wake of World War II.

The second part of the chapter urges IR scholarship on international history to transcend the reiteration of and reliance on 'substantialist' concepts
about the Concert system. At the same time, it calls for reengaging with and
encountering the content, practices, and patterns of the very interactions
that prompted their emergence in the first place. Such an account presents
the occurrences at the Congress as a vibrant and unpredictable dance. At
Vienna, each participant performed multiple roles, scripted by the various
diplomatic dances in which they found themselves entangled. The waltz
prompted movements and relations, which framed the diplomatic interactions of the Congress. The Concert system is thereby a shorthand for the
kind of dancing relationality that took place in the ballrooms of Vienna and
the community that it engendered. It refers not merely to the actors that
it connects (be they diplomatic representatives or states), but rather to the
entanglements that act on and in between these actors.

The point here is that although several important critiques of the standard IR narrative about the Concert of Europe have emerged, almost all of
them tend to subscribe – and often reify – its substantialist assumptions. In
this respect, the extant critique tends to offer qualifications to some of the
narrative elements, but fails to offer a relational alternative to the accepted
account of the Congress of Vienna and its consequences. This chapter
therefore evidences an attempt to recall the relationality – and, in particular, the social practices, reciprocal figurations, and personal interconnections – which have been carefully excluded from the standard narrative.
To the extent that it functioned, the Concert system was a contingent social

practice made possible by fluid iterations of social transactions that percolated and gained salience in the context of ongoing and multiple relations during the nine months of the Congress. What mattered in this setting were the roles engendered by the interactions at Vienna and which the participants played in the context of their interactions. The Concert was thereby (and ultimately) undone by the breakdown of this relationality. The relationality of the Concert system was separate from (and more than the sum of) the rationalities of the participating actors.

In other words, the 'international' so conceived emerges as a relational system brimming with social interactions rather than withdrawal from such exchanges. This contrasts with the interactions at the 'international' level prescribed by the standard account. Informed by a Cartesian bifurcation between self and other, the situational context of international interactions predisposes great powers and small powers alike to act in a predictable manner – namely, the relational context transforms generic fears into specific threats either for the purposes of alliance building or providing opportunities for conquest (Cesa 2014: 19–20). Such an account then backstops an atomistic reading of global life focused on sovereign states (and, especially, the 'significant' ones – i.e., the great power), who pursue competing interests in an international system characterized by anarchy and structured by power. Consequently, even though global life is complex, it can be studied in substantialist terms. The relational dancing of the Congress contests this narrative by suggesting that the turbulence characterizing international affairs can be neither predicted nor measured. Just like the waltz, whose movements are always already different, global life not only moves in mysterious ways, but in the process it transforms, changes, and adapts in ways that cannot be anticipated in advance (and whose very patterns and practices adjust and change continuously and unexpectedly).

Notes

1 See Lascurettes (2017) for an overview of the literature on different 'concerts of democracies'.
2 Curiously, Ross Hoffman (1941: 683) insists that the pragmatism of the Concert of Europe derived neither from any 'general principles' nor particular 'ideological conceptions'.
3 Francis Harry Hinsley reinforces this point by asserting that 'the impressive thing about the behaviour of the Powers in 1815 is that they were prepared, as they had never previously been prepared to waive their individual interests because it was in their individual interests to do so' (Hinsley 1963: 7).
4 A number of commentators emphasize this point by indicating that 'the impressive thing about the behaviour of the Powers in 1815 is that they were prepared as they had never previously been prepared to waive their individual interests in the pursuit of an international system' (Hinsley 1963: 97).

5 Castlereagh's injunction is quite instructive in this regard: 'The great military Powers of the Continent who have triumphed in the War, should recollect, that they avowedly fought for *their own liberties, and for those of the rest of Europe, and not for an extension of their dominion[s]* . . . If the Allied Powers act liberally towards each other, and indulgently to other states, they may look forward to crown a glorious war by a solid, and lasting peace, and posterity will revere their names, not only for having delivered by their arms the world from a tyrant and conqueror, but for having restored, by their example and by their influence, the reign of moderation and justice' (quoted in Jarrett 2013: 68; emphasis added).

6 The whole episode is discussed in Sinsheimer (2016: 185–186).

7 The 'Eastern Question' is largely associated with the rise of nationalism across the Ottoman Empire and the weakening capacity of the Ottoman state to maintain the polity together. The key issue in the conversations on the Eastern Question was the future (ownership) of the territories occupied by the Ottoman Empire (Kavalski 2008).

8 The term 'deep hanging out' refers to immersive practices and methodologies of research and encounter associated with the work of anthropologist Clifford Geertz (1998).

9 This point is developed in the following section.

10 It should not be overlooked that to a significant degree the popularity of the waltz derived from the fact that it was the first dance that allowed touching between the opposite sexes.

11 In fact, in an earlier diplomatic iteration of the term 'concert', the French representative to the Treaty of Utrecht, Charles-Irénée Castel, abbé de Saint-Pierre, argued for the establishment of a European concert precisely because it would provide 'the great security to Christians against the inroads of the Turk' and offer a united front 'to chase the Turks out of Europe' (quoted in Mastnak 2003: 225–228; see also Ramel 2014: 132).

2 The relational turn(s) in the Anglosphere and Sinosphere of international relations

Introduction

The reference to a 'relational turn' in the title of this chapter is obviously a misnomer. All modes of theorizing account for relation and have specific kinds of interactions in mind for their explanation and understanding. In fact, most modes of knowledge production would fit quite comfortably within a 'larger family of *relational social theory*' (Jackson and Nexon 2017: 1; emphasis in original). However, the reference to a relational turn here is associated with the work in the mid-1990s of what some have labelled 'the New York School' of relational sociology (Mische 2011: 80–98). Although the main aim of this school of relational sociology seems to have been the trouncing of the antinomies between structure and agency by exploring the dynamics of social interactions, some of its proponents also aspired to establishing 'a comprehensive paradigmatic way of taking social structure seriously by studying directly how patterns of ties allocate resources in a social system' (Wellman 1998: 20). Trickling into IR by the end of the 1990s, this mode of relational inquiry has been associated with the seminal work by Patrick Thaddeus Jackson and Daniel H. Nexon (1999) – both of them 'products' of this 'New York School'. Consequently, more often than not, the claim to a *relational* mode of IR inquiry is either directly inspired by their work or emerges as a critical response.

At the same time, relationality in IR has gradually grown into prominence – perhaps, paradoxically, not least because of its simultaneous 'uncovery' and appropriation by both the Anglophone and Sinophone (as well as speaking more broadly, the so-called Western and non-Western) approaches. Although relationality has been mentioned in the literature earlier (Baumgartner et al. 1975; Richardson 1956), it seems that the two sides of this conversation take the 1999 article by Jackson and Nexon as the starting point for their investigations. Thus, this chapter's reference to a 'relational turn' in IR is a reflection of the intellectual interactions and oeuvre connected with this trend both in the Anglosphere and Sinosphere of IR. As will be elaborated in the following sections, the transformative potential of relationalism (not only for IR) derives from its suggestion that 'things' do not exist *prior to* and *outside of* relations – that is, actors/entities emerge in the process of interactions, and their identities and interests will be different in different spaces and times. For instance (and with the danger of oversimplification), the China that interacts with the United States is a different actor (i.e., it plays different roles) from the China that interacts with Kazakhstan because of different historical and reciprocal experiences; at the same time, the China that has interacted with the United States in 1980 is different from the China that has interacted with the United States in 1990, 2000, or 2010, despite certain continuities in its strategic culture – namely, because such continuities gain different inflections and interpretations in each of their temporal iterations. In other words,

> The 'relational turn' attends broadly to relationship-embedded role identities that motivate the quest for recognition, exertion of self-restraint, and normative role taking, as opposed to the pursuit of interests, resort to self-help, and interventionary enforcement. The relational turn asks why and how national actors can make and take roles, incorporate collective identities, and act on behalf of an imagined entity greater than the nation in itself. The relational turn is particularly suitable for the analysis of non-competitive relationships, in which national actors do not seek to gain anything particular or immediate from each other. Without largely non-competitive relationships in the background, nations would not be able to concentrate on the rather few security agendas that make up contemporary IR research.
>
> (Shih 2016: 2)

The following part of this chapter details the claims of the main proponents of the relational turn in the Anglosphere and Sinosphere of IR. The first section looks at the conversation in the Anglophone literature. The focus here is on the work of Patrick Thaddeus Jackson and Daniel H. Nexon and Louiza Odysseos. The second section outlines the Sinophone accounts of relationality. The focus is on the work of Qin Yaqing and Zhao Tingyang. As it will be explained, the selected representatives are neither the sole interlocutors, nor do they cover the full spectrum of relational perspectives either in the Anglophone or Sinophone strands of IR, let alone in the myriad other linguistic and cultural traditions of world affairs. Instead, the selected authors represent key nodes in the respective conversations on relationality. At the same time, the labels of Anglophone and Sinophone do not impute coherence among the interlocutors of relationality in either of these linguistic traditions. Thus, even though some ascertain that 'Western relationality is a process of becoming synchronized, whereas Chinese relationality is one of staying accepted' (Shih 2016: 7), this research does not inhere with such assertions.

Relationality in Anglophone IR

Anglophone IR covers a wide and intractable terrain dotted with disparate theoretical perspectives and various groupings of interlocutors. Yet some assert that its Anglophone discourse is plagued by a 'castle syndrome' – proponents of different IR schools engage in defending and reinforcing the bulwarks of their analytical castles, while bombarding the claims of everybody else (Barkin 2010; Kavalski 2007). The contention is that the discipline has increasingly immersed itself in debates on the substantiation of particular paradigms rather than engaging with the fluidity of global life. To put it bluntly, the turbulence of world affairs appears to have relevance (primarily) to the extent that it can validate (or disprove) the proposition of a particular IR school. Such contention should not be misunderstood as a condemnation of the field or as a suggestion that it lacks sophistication. On the contrary, post–Cold War developments have challenged the discipline to venture into intellectual terrains that it previously did not deem necessary, or important, or worthwhile. The contention here is that while this has been going on, IR scholars failed to break from the substantialist leftover mode of thinking in paradigms – probably one of the most palpable Cold War legacies of the discipline. Thus, despite the 'new challenges', the IR mainstream has not abandoned its 'old habits' (Waltz 2002). Such a proclivity has recently been termed 'returnism' – IR's predilection for traditional conceptual signposts that provide intellectual comfort zones but are 'simply images of old concepts' de-contextualized from (and, therefore, inapplicable to) current realities (Heng 2010).

In this respect, although Anglophone IR is populated by different kinds of relational inquiry, such investigations seem to rarely abandon the substantialist premise of their atomistic metanarrative. In fact, one of the main critiques of Anglophone modalities of relationality is that they remain 'locked into a framework that posits an identity horizon (organizational conservation) for (structural) change' (Protevi 2013: 21). Such proclivity to 'entity-seeking' (Jackson and Nexon 1999) then presages conceptualizations that are both explicitly and (especially) implicitly underpinned by assertions that emphasize 'how identities arise from *interaction* and how these identities in turn are important for actions and more generally for dynamics in the international system' (Bucher 2012: 3; emphasis added). The following sections detail the propositions of two of the main interlocutors of the conversation on relationality in Anglophone IR: (1) Patrick Thaddeus Jackson and Daniel H. Nexon and (2) Louiza Odysseos. There are others, but the works of these two sets of authors seems to resonate most prominently within the relational turn in IR. Also, a final qualification is in order: for the purposes of clarity, the critique of these two sets of relational perspectives appears in the endnotes to this chapter rather than in the main body of the text.

The processual relationalism of Patrick Thaddeus Jackson and Daniel H. Nexon

The relational turn proposed by Patrick Thaddeus Jackson and Daniel H. Nexon (1999) takes as its point of departure the manifesto of the sociologist Mustafa Emirbayer. Drawing on his work they sketch the nascent outlines of the IR research agenda on relationality. In fact, their initial salvo can be read as an act of translation – translating Emirbayer's sociological propositions to the language of IR. The point of departure for Jackson and Nexon is the investigation of what would happen to the knowledge production of IR were we to deploy Emirbayer's distinction between 'substantialist' and 'relational' theorizing. The former posits that 'entities', 'things', and 'substances' are the ontological priors of global life, whereas the latter treats 'interactions', 'relations', and 'transactions' as the starting points of observation, explanation, and understanding. Thus, whereas substantialism suggests that relations occur only between different entities (primarily 'states' according to IR) and that interactions have no agential quality beyond the subjectivity and intentionality of the actors involved in these exchanges, relationalism asserts that it is interactions that produce actors (and it would be better to refer to these as 'figurations of ties') and ushers in a much more dynamic and contingent outlook on global life (Jackson and Nexon 1999: 282). The point here is that substantialism takes entities as the main unit of analysis and relationalism takes interactions.

Jackson and Nexon contend that the bulk of theory building in IR – including all the main orthodoxies (and their variants) – affiliates with the substantialist camp. In this respect, substantialism – in particular, the belief that actors precede and are formed outside of the dynamics of interaction – appears to be the common denominator 'cut[ting] across conventional divisions in the field, including theories in all the major "paradigms" of IR' (Jackson and Nexon 1999: 293). Due to these commitments, the IR conversation has tended to privilege issues of epistemology and methodology (and occasionally ethics), but lacks any kind of ontological pluralism. Therefore, it is not surprising that most IR analyses tend to prioritize 'states' as the main (and often only) actors on the world stage and treat them as self-same entities – both functionally the same 'like units' and unchangeable, regardless of their international interactions. What might potentially change according to this substantialist account are some of the attributes of statehood, but not their constitutive properties (Jackson and Nexon 1999: 293). Consequently, and regardless of their theoretical commitment, IR scholars purvey visions of 'the world out there' as a closed system populated by sovereign states, whose interactions are motivated by power maximization and the pursuit of their own self-interest. The framework of instrumental-rational action has thus become the standard against which alternative claims are judged. The 'atomistic ontology' of substantialism asserts that all social phenomena are quantifiable and predictable (Kurki 2008: 17). Given the linear causality backstopping the substantialist metanarrative, as well as a result of the prevalence of reductionist models postulating that all physical phenomena change in a gradual manner and following foreseeable trajectories, what comes to pass in world affairs is presented as subject to anticipation. Apart from relaying on over-generalizations, such substantialism tends to purvey profoundly essentializing claims about the actors, factors, and processes animating international politics. Not surprisingly, global life tends to be envisioned as a domain of disconnected states, infamously imagined by Arnold Wolfers (1962: 19) as billiard balls – 'closed, impermeable, and sovereign unit[s], completely separated from all other states'.

In this setting, relationalism offers both a viable and a much-needed alternative to the dominance of substantialism in IR. As many have pointed out, IR's investment in 'egotistic, autonomous actors' is nothing short of an enchantment with 'a fiction of Enlightenment philosophy' (Lebow 2003: 360). Due to the dynamism of interactions, Jackson and Nexon label their approach as 'processual relationalism' (Jackson and Nexon 1999: 292). This is a transactional approach that takes sociality as prior – both logically and in practice – to the actors engaged in interactions. From this perspective, it is increasingly difficult to imagine global life as 'billiard balls slamming into another series of billiard balls'; instead, it 'look[s] much more like reverberations along a web of interdependencies' (Jackson and Nexon 1999: 299).

To assist the operationalization of processual relationalism, Jackson and Nexon elaborate four elements – *processes, configurations, projects*, and *yoking* (Jackson and Nexon 1999: 301). The emphasis on *processes* seeks to disrupt the ways in which change is construed in IR. In particular, Jackson and Nexon aim to demonstrate that change is endogenous to the patterns of international relations and the ways these are theorized in IR. Due to the substantialism that pervades IR, change is nearly invariably exogenous and associated customarily with some form of agential intentionality – namely, an international actor purposefully acts in a particular way that triggers a series of reactions from others that cumulatively lead to a change in the broader patters of relations. In contrast to such understanding, processual relationalism proposes that causality in international interactions does not have to always be associated with a specific actor doing something on the world stage. Instead, many things happen in world affairs not only independent of the actors involved, but very often it is these happenings that disclose the 'actorness' and 'subjectivity' of those entangled in the dynamics of interaction. In this respect, the processes of international relations can be described as 'un-owned' and elicit 'doings' which are not attributable to a particular 'doer' (Jackson and Nexon 1999: 302). The circles of reciprocal implication revealed by processual relationalism suggest that world affairs should be considered a contingent and dynamic domain of ongoing change where causality and subjectivity emerge as figurations of circumstance and interaction.

In this setting, *configurations* have to be understood as 'aggregations of processes' providing contingent interactive contexts of 'relational differences which give rise to meaningful action' (Jackson and Nexon 1999: 304). Within processual relationalism, the utility of configurations for the purposes of knowledge production is twofold: (1) in terms of explanation, configurations help to 'distinguish between the process which is the object of analysis and the processes which are treated as primitives for the sake of the particular analysis'; and (2) in terms of understanding, configurations provide 'systems of meaning . . . generated by narrative and dialogue' which assist with the construction of causal stories (albeit not of a linear kind) about the 'symbolic technologies' constitutive of the practices of international politics (Jackson and Nexon 1999: 304–306). Configurations thus offer insights into the circumstances and contingencies that go into the relational production of the processes of international interactions.

The third element of the processual relationalism proposed by Jackson and Nexon is *projects*. Projects denote 'a configuration with agent properties, a social entity with the ability to make choices and exercise causal power' (Jackson and Nexon 1999: 307). At the heart of such preoccupation with projects within the framework of processual relationalism is the examination of 'what agents *are* and how their agency is produced and sustained' (Jackson and Nexon 1999: 308). Thus, in contrast to substantialist fixation with the activities of individual international actors, relational analysis draws attention to the emergence and behaviour of different international actors in the context of the diversity of relations that enmesh and interpenetrate them. It is important to acknowledge that in this framing, projects are not taken to be self-organizing but goal motivated. As Jackson and Nexon suggest, a project is distinguished

> by the fact that it unfolds, or at least tries to unfold, according to some generic plan; the plan *is* the unity of the project, lending interpretative

coherence to the various actions which make up the project. Without this overall goal, the various activities would be meaningless.

(Jackson and Nexon 1999: 316)

Actorness makes sense only in terms of its production and constitution through webs of reciprocal implication. Rather than a distinct property of individual international actors, the key qualities of projects are a function of circumstances and contingent on the particular spatial and temporal specificity of interactions. Such engagement with the relational ramifications of projects suggests that actors are continuously being produced and reproduced through interactions.

Finally, in order to frame the ways in which certain 'configurations are reified into entities, and how these entities in turn come to manifest agentic properties', Jackson and Nexon turn to the concept of *yoking* (Jackson and Nexon 1999: 312). Drawing on the social theory of Andrew Abbott, they employ the notion of yoking to outline the relational dynamics that bring actors into existence. Jackson and Nexon acknowledge that relational analyses find it hard to conceptualize 'things' – that is, are entities mere accidents, 'a kind of a standing wave', or something else altogether (Jackson and Nexon 1999: 313)? According to them, such analytical posers reveal the persistence of rationalist methodologies and, in particular, the attempts to devise theories of social interaction fitting the criteria of willed action and self-conscious directionality. In relational approaches such coherence is rare (if at all possible). Instead, actorness is contingent on contextual interactions over time. The notion of yoking assists with the elaboration of these dynamics. In particular, it underscores that

> the work of creating an entity must also be seen as the work of rationalizing [in the sense of formalizing] various connections so that the resulting entity has the ability to endure as a persistent thing, in the various ecologies in which it is located.
>
> (Abbott 1996a: 870–872; Jackson and Nexon 1999: 314)

In terms of the framework of processual relationalism, yoking performs two important functions: (1) first, rather than a static condition, actorness emerges as a dynamic process 'involving the persistent drawing and redrawing of boundaries, establishing and re-establishing those demarcations which make it possible to speak of entities'; (2) second, the intentionality of agency is not a subjective and/or psychological process, but a matter of public and contextual practices of interaction, though which the meaning of an action is engendered (Jackson and Nexon 1999: 315). Thus, yoking seems to simultaneously be a causal configuration and an unintended consequence of interaction (Jackson and Nexon 1999: 317).

The relational coexistence of Louiza Odysseos

The other major treatment of relationality in IR is associated with the work of Louiza Odysseos (2007). Just like Jackson and Nexon, she asserts that most of what we take to be IR orthodoxy is indelibly marked by a profound and utter disinterest in the question of relationality. In particular, her work reconsiders the concepts and practices of coexistence in world politics. Taking IR's ontology of separation as her point of departure, Odysseos observes that mainstream accounts treat the concept and practices of coexistence merely as coterminous with co-presence – that is, the parallel existence (co-dwelling) of two or more actors. Yet despite interacting with one another, this account of coexistence is defined by its 'nonrelationality' (Odysseos 2007: xxv). For Odysseos, this is symptomatic of the articulation of the modern subject in continental political thought as a ' "being without relations" . . . perfectly detached, distinct, and closed . . . it is unencumbered; it is solitary; it is unaffected' (Odysseos 2007: xxviii). Thus, coexistence is usually presented as a function of residing 'side by side: it does not require that we live together in any meaningful way; it merely records that we live in the same limited space' (Odysseos 2007: xvi). The world stage then becomes a domain populated by 'nonrelational and self-sufficient subjects' whose interactions 'must be composed in mere collaboration of the same physical space' (Odysseos 2007: 178). In this setting, coexistence grows to be understood as the opposite of conflict: (1) first, coexistence facilitates the transcendence of conflict; and (2) second, it enables survival in an anarchical world. The association of nonrelational co-presence with 'the nexus of survival' is turned into a particularly potent analytical lens during the Cold War when the possibility of 'nuclear annihilation served to affirm and highlight the assumed opposition of coexistence and conflict' (Odysseos 2007: xiv).

It is this intellection and historical legacy that then provide the foundations both for IR's neglect of coexistence and for treating it not as 'the *primary* condition in which entities find themselves' but as 'a state that must be actively, and secondarily, brought about' (Odysseos 2007: xv; emphasis in original). Thus, due to its framing as a post-ontological and derivative condition which emerges from the purposive and intentional interactions of self-conscious actors, IR research tends to block out the act, practices, and state of coexistence in order so that it can keep on privileging investigation favouring the conditions under which actors are willing to move away from the allegedly principal dynamics of conflict as a viable strategy for ensuring their survival. In this setting, coexistence is taken to refer only to 'a technical issue of how to arrange units in a certain manner to bring about this condition of togetherness crucial to "survival" ' (Odysseos 2007: xxix). During the Cold War, this understanding came to define IR's central claim that 'the international' represents 'a violence-steeped state of nature' (Odysseos 2007: 23). Survival, therefore, becomes 'the predominant relational schema of IR – it offers 'a *particular* kind of relationality whose focus is the protection of the self and the surviving of the other' (Odysseos 2007: 21). In this setting, coexistence is reduced to an enabler of survival, which restricts the understanding of 'relationality to mere co-presence of preconstituted entities' (Odysseos 2007: xxii).

Normatively speaking then, within the substantialist account, violence (and its potential) are not only an endemic feature of international affairs, but a desirable one. In other words, the notion and practices of ethics have a rather constrained role on foreign policy. Therefore, as Martin Wight has acknowledged, a quote from Joseph de Maistre deserves 'a mark over some other candidates for not misrepresenting the historical record' of world politics because of its ability to capture the discrete and self-interested international agency of sovereign states:

> The whole earth, continually drenched with blood, is nothing but an immense altar where all living things must be sacrificed without end, and without limit, and without ceasing, until the consummation of all things, until evil is extinguished, and until death itself is dead.
> (Wight 1960: 62; 1977: 12–13)

In an analytical vein redolent of Jackson and Nexon, Odysseos finds fault with the dominant framing of sovereign statehood in IR. Yet although her analysis targets the construction of states as unitary, self-determining subjects prior to (and outside of) processes of interaction in a manner similar to that of Jackson and Nexon, Odysseos does not seek to offer a relational reading of the state. Instead, her main preoccupation remains squarely with the concept and practices of coexistence; on the other hand, Odysseos seeks to demonstrate such framing as a strategy for surviving all kinds of 'others' and, on the other hand, to disrupt it. This understanding reflects the nonrelational underpinnings of IR – namely, that enmity is omnipresent on the world stage and that all actors are, by definition, enemies (Odysseos 2007: 19–24). According to Odysseos, the resultant understanding of coexistence as a nonrelational co-presence hinders IR's capacity for thinking through the question of relationality. In other words, if IR is to engage meaningfully the transformative possibilities of relationality, it has to reassess its own ontology and that of its take on modern subjectivity.

Drawing on the work of Martin Heidegger, Emmanuel Levinas, and Jean-Luc Nancy, Odysseos decries the 'ontological totalitarianism' of mainstream IR (Odysseos 2007: 50) and outlines a relationality which shifts the discourse away from survival towards coexistence and which is able to see the possibility of interactions between the (Western) self and its many others, free from the structures of mastery, domination, and conflict. Her critique targets the assumption that relations are self-evidently *secondary* to the *primary* condition of conflict on the world stage, which then legitimizes the post-ontological assertion that peaceful coexistence is possible only through the complete mastery and subjugation of all forms of otherness (i.e., 'domination over everything which is not itself') (Odysseos 2007: xxxi). In contrast, relationality – as a concept and practice – 'illuminates an account of existence as coexistence, as permeated through and through by otherness' (Odysseos 2007: 57). Such radical embeddedness in a world made of and by interactions discloses relationality as an ontologically prior and primary capacity of the subject (be that an individual or a state) (Odysseos 2007: 75). Odysseos therefore rearticulates relationality as 'Being-in-the-world *with others*' (Odysseos 2007: 59; emphasis in original).[1]

Because international actors are always and only in relations, 'the international' is neither distinct nor removed from these interactions. Instead, it remains 'an object of possible interpretation' (Odysseos 2007: 84). These interpretations are subject to the contingent moods that grip the participants engaged in interaction. To assist with this reconsideration, Odysseos proposes 'heteronomy' as a substitute for the 'autonomy' trope dominating the narratives and purview of IR; in particular, it is the preoccupation with sovereign autonomy which provides the foundation for a security-seeking behaviour motivated by the pursuit of a complete 'mastery over otherness' or a strife for 'domination over everything which is not itself' (Odysseos 2007: xxx). Such a move allows her to recover a relational mode of coexistence in which selfhood and otherness are in 'a relation other than that of opposition itself, a relation of differential intrication' (Odysseos 2007: xxx). In this heteronomous framing, coexistence is no longer presented as a mere stand-in for unrelational co-presence, but discloses an active attitude (and aptitude) for 'being-other-directed' as well as 'being-radically-in-relation' (Odysseos 2007: xxxi). Consequently, in what is presented as a relational pattern of world affairs, international actors are disclosed as 'coexistentially heteronomous beings' (Odysseos 2007: xxxii). This means that they are always and already social and 'wholly indebted to the other' for their 'self-understanding and for the meanings and orientations' that these actors have 'of, and within, the world [they] inhabit' (Odysseos 2007: 30).[2]

For Odysseos, relationality suggests 'withness' – a 'prior [and dispositional] capacity of actors "to-be-with" others', which makes interactions possible in the first place (Odysseos 2007: 71–74). She calls this capacity 'the optics of coexistence' – a 'coexistential heteronomy' which attests to the relational character of subjectivity 'immersed continuously among things and other beings' and enabling 'a different *seeing* of the phenomena of existence' (Odysseos 2007: 58). Such optics of coexistence suggest that an actor and its international behaviour as well as 'the norms and rules that help it go about its business in the world are structured by others and are only shared by [that actors]' (Odysseos 2007: 59). Relationality thus defined reframes the international as 'a web of involvements with other beings' and populated by actors who are neither perceived as, nor perceive themselves to be, autonomous, assertive, and masterful, but are radically embedded in the world (Odysseos 2007: 57–66).[3]

Relationality with Chinese characteristics

Many have asserted that although the commitment to relationality is new for most contemporary IR theories, Chinese intellectual traditions have long been defined by a normative commitment to relationalism, which makes them uniquely positioned to provide significant contributions to the global field of IR (Zhang 2016: 180). At the same time, the perceived difficulty of the disciplinary mainstream to articulate a relational IR has drawn substantive criticism from a number of Chinese IR scholars. Most prominently, Qin Yaqing (2009: 3) has used it to evidence his claim that the Anglosphere of IR's mainstream lacks a theory of relations.[4] Such stance reflects a long line of Chinese intellectual suspicions of Western knowledge production, not least because of the violence it meted out on the non-West in the wake of the Congress of Vienna. For instance, the Chinese reformist and scholar, Liang Qichao (梁啟超, 1873–1929), while drawing on and translating the work of European scholars, insisted that '[t]he Westerners were very self-conceited. They thought the world only belonged to them' (quoted in Gao 2008: 201).

Generally speaking, Chinese contributions to the conversation on relationality in the study and practices of world affairs tend to sit within the broader context of non-Eurocentric or post-Western perspectives in IR. The broad commitment of these perspectives is not only about the lack of relationality in the Anglophone/Eurocentric mainstream, but rather that the forms of relationality and interaction that are allowed to be fostered are 'limited to those (inter)actions that can be understood to be in line with the reproduction or circulation of – a particular rendering of – political life and political order(ing)' (Ansems de Vries 2015: 72). At the same time, others assert that 'Chinese relationality is about anxiety instead of passion' (Shih 2016: 2). Perhaps a central feature that a number of the proponents of relationality in Sinophone IR share is that they tend to resort to the ancient

Chinese thought for their explanation and understanding (Ling 2015; Shih 2016; 207; Zhang 2015, 2016). This section focuses on two of the main proponents of relationality in Sinophone IR: Qin Yaqing and Zhao Tingyang. Again, before delving into their arguments, it would be useful to remind that just like in the previous section, the critique of Qin's and Zhao's take on relationality appears in the endnotes to this chapter.

The relational theory of world politics of Qin Yaqing

Much of the excitement and innovation associated with relationality in Chinese IR has been associated with the seminal work of Qin Yaqing (秦亚青).
In fact, his effort and insights have given impetus to much of the ongoing rethinking of the theories and practices of relationality across the various locales of global IR. It has to be stated at the outset that while making a distinct and important contribution, Qin frames his engagement with relationality as a response to (and, significantly, a critique of) the work of Jackson and Nexon (as well as the endeavours of their intellectual mentor Emirbayer). To cut a long story short, Qin finds problems both with the metanarrative and the analytical framework of their processual relationalism. On the one hand, even though he concurs (and even affiliates) with Jackson and Nexon (and their followers) that the mainstream theories of IR ignore the significance of social interactions, Qin faults processual relationalism for its underlying commitment to 'Western rationalism' (Qin 2009: 14). According to Qin, the inability to problematize the Eurocentric roots of IR's substantialism invariably hems in the endeavours of Jackson and Nexon. This leads them to propound an equally Eurocentric, isolated (and isolationist) 'relations-for-relations sake' approach as that of the substantionalism they seek to expose. The broader critique is that processual relationalism fails to decentre the monological knowledge production of IR. Thus, the exclusion (and expulsion) of 'non-Western' perspectives and experiences perpetuated from this account of relationality fails to trouble the underlying 'individualistic rationality' (of substantialist IR) – which Qin defines as the underlying 'metaphysical component of the theoretical hard core' of Eurocentric IR (Qin 2016: 34).

On the other hand, Qin criticizes the processual relationalism that Jackson and Nexon propose because of its seeming inability to distinguish between 'relations and processes' and taking the latter to be equivalent with the former (Qin 2009). In this setting, the relationality that Jackson and Nexon propound seems unable to escape the requirement for an 'external push' that sets off interactions and makes it possible to account for 'the internal dynamism of the process' (Qin 2009: 14). In this respect, processual relationalism can be seen merely as a means to realize cost efficiency on the world stage, rather than as a volitional and committed practice 'that is historical and socio-cultural, defining a community and shaping the behaviour of its members' (Qin 2011: 137).

In contrast, to these engagements, Qin takes the relational complexity of international society as the point of departure for his investigations. Drawing on Chinese intellectual traditions – especially, Confucianism – he sets off to articulate a distinctly Chinese relational theory of world politics. His point of departure is the assertion that relationality is the defining characteristic of Chinese thought and practice. The social embeddedness in interactions has 'always been given the first priority in the Chinese mindset', and it is thereby the natural pivot and the basic unit of social analysis (Qin 2009: 9). In this respect, it is the processes of ongoing relations that produce 'social meaning' through the practice of interactions – namely, it is relations that 'shape an actor's identity and influence her behaviour' (Qin 2009: 9). In this framing, processes represent 'an open becoming with unlimited possibilities'; at the same time, the forces animating these interactions gain their 'own life through the unfolding and dynamic relations among actors' (Qin 2016: 37). The implication from these assertions is threefold: (1) first, agents and processes are mutually constitutive – 'agents constitute process through their action or interaction, while process exerts constraining and enabling effects on agents'; (2) second, social processes craft intersubjectivity – understood as 'sets of social practices and relational processes that give interactions meaning'; intersubjectivity provides the relational rules and norms that animate 'the dynamism of the ego-alter relationship'; (3) third, all social actors are embedded in (and impossible to construe as agents outside of) the process and practices of purposeful interaction (Qin 2009: 9–10).

On this premise, Qin goes on to envisage global life as a 'complex network of flowing relations', in which 'each line or knot of relational network moves, generating dynamics for the process. However, the dynamics itself cannot be reduced to any single line or knot of the network' (Qin 2009: 11–12).[5] The assertion that the whole is more than the sum of its parts, then, informs the constitutive assumptions of Qin's relational theory of IR. The first one is that 'relationality has ontological significance' (Qin 2009: 14). The suggestion is that 'the IR world is a universe of interrelatedness' (Qin 2016: 35). Abandoning substantialist commitments to individualism has a direct bearing on the framing of 'the social context composed by relations' (Qin 2009: 16). In particular, such perspective urges rearticulating the international society as 'a relational web' whose dynamics are embedded in and emerge from the contingent figurations of interaction. Such position informs a context-oriented international society which represents the world as a 'complexly related whole' whose social vitality is 'defined by the fundamental relatedness of all to all' (Qin 2016: 36).

The second assumption of Qin's relational theory of world politics is that 'relations define identity' (Qin 2009: 15). The point here is that 'actors are and can only be "actors-in-relations"', and social relations have a shaping power over their identity formation (Qin 2016: 38). The assertion that social actors do not exist outside of the context of social relations proffers a dynamic understanding of identity as a relationally circumstantial construct. Drawing on Chinese intellectual traditions, Qin posits that in contrast to the Eurocentric rootedness of identity in the dictum of 'cogito ergo sum', Chinese takes on identity reflect an understanding that 'there is no me in isolation to be considered abstractly: I am the totality of roles I live in relation to specific others' (Qin 2016: 36). Such contingent framing suggests that identity is 'by nature, multifold, interactive, and changeable along with practice' (Qin 2009: 16). Qin's claim then is that 'individuals *per se* have no identities'; instead, 'identity and relational webs co-exist, co-define, and co-transform' (Qin 2009: 15–16).[6]

The third assumption of Qin's relational theory of world politics is that power is relational – it is not a property of any one actor, but is relationally engendered by, in, and through the dynamics of social interactions. Qin's reckoning with the relational nature of power emphasizes that 'it is nurtured and defined in the relational web' (Qin 2009: 17). What this means is that rather than a material possession or an equation of capabilities, power becomes a contingent reflection of intersubjective and circumstantial relational practices. It is in the ongoing iterations of such practices that actors 'constantly manipulate and manage [their] relational circles. An actor is more powerful because she has larger relational circles, more intimate and important others in these circles, and more social prestige because of these circles' (Qin 2016: 42). In this setting, 'relations are power' and 'relations always influence [enlarge and/ or constrain] the exercise of power' (Qin 2009: 16–18). The inference here is that what actors are after is not influence (in the sense of power over others, which tends to be associated with the logic of control underpinning the concept and practices of both hard and soft power [and their many variants]), but ensuring the longevity of relations by reinforcing the strength of ties through ongoing commitment to and active participation in interactions. The crucial inflection is that the currency of relational power is 'social capital such as face/reputation' (Qin 2016: 42).

In this setting, Qin outlines the 'logic of relationship' animating his relational theory of world politics. The intention is to emphasize the framing effects of sociality on actors' relational capacities. The point of departure for such logic of relationality is the observation that 'an actor tends to make decisions according to the degrees of intimacy and/or importance of her relationships to specific others, with the totality of her relational circles as the background' (Qin 2016: 37). Thus, in contrast to mainstream accounts which assume that actors are distinct and separate from one another, the logic of relationality insists that 'things or variables change along with the change of their relations; individuals in the web are subject to changes in the relational web as a whole; and, similarly, the interaction among individuals can have an impact on the web' (Qin 2009: 15). Consequently, and methodologically speaking, a relational logic of inquiry would not try to control variables and demand substantive isolation of temporal and causal factors; instead, it would seek to offer a comprehensive engagement with the overall context of interactions by embracing its complexity and taking into account as many variables as possible into the investigation. The messiness and unpredictability of interactions suggests that the 'relational totality constitutes a social context, which shapes and is shaped by, enables and is enabled by, and constrains and is constrained by actors' (Qin 2016: 38).[7]

According to Qin, the logic of relationality works in two distinct directions. First, 'relations select' – meaning that 'it is relational circles in which an actor is embedded that enable and constrain her behaviour' (Qin 2016: 38). The implication is that in a complex world, the logic of relationships takes precedence over the logic of consequences and the logic of appropriateness informing mainstream approaches to IR. It is the very totality of social relations that not only defines what is rational and appropriate, but also 'precludes abstract individual rationality and self-sustained agency, which assumes the ability of discrete individuals to make decisions on the basis of self-interest' (Qin 2016: 38). The key inflection here is the centrality of the social context – it is the very circumstances of interaction that act as the '[invisible] hand that orients an actor toward a certain action' (Qin 2016: 38).

Second, the logic of relationality works in the direction of relational circles and insists that these are utilized for instrumental purposes. This element comes to indicate that relational action can be and, more often than not, is self-interested. This comes as a corrective to the altruistic underpinnings of Odysseos' claim that relational actors are other-oriented; other-oriented behaviour does not have to be altruistic – relationality is a self-interested (though not selfish) interactive strategy. In this sense, social actors utilize their 'relational circles to facilitate the achievement of instrumental objectives' (Qin 2016: 38). What might appear as the instrumental direction of the logic of relationality can be employed for the achievement of 'immediate payoffs' or 'longer term returns', or 'even merely for social capital as reputation and prestige' (Qin 2016: 38). At the same time, such instrumentality can be deployed 'for achieving and maintaining social order' (Qin 2016: 38). By virtue both of their location in a dynamic social context and perceiving the world as a complex non-additive composition of ongoing relations, relational actors do not seek to merge into a homogenous international society, but aspire for the dialogical management of their differences through interaction so that these do not lead 'to conflict and disorder, but on the contrary, can add up to stability' (Qin 2016: 39). The logic of relationality is integral to Qin's outline of global order. According to him, mainstream Western accounts of order are marked by their 'rule-based' governmentality. The ontological premise of such narratives is that the world stage is populated by disconnected international actors. This proposition calls for regulation of the behaviour of such detached and egotistical entities. Rules thereby provide the convenient rational model for the management of such self-regarding actors by providing instrumental and normative prescriptions (as well as proscriptions) for their behaviour. It is the formalization of rules both through international institutions and as ethical standards that ensures the predictability of international interactions. It is also the guidance of such rule-based framework that makes it possible to speak of international society in world politics. As Qin puts it succinctly, 'because actors are egoists and, therefore, are not trustworthy, they make and trust rules instead of trusting one another' (Qin 2016: 43). In contrast, the relational framing of global order 'focuses on the governing of relations among actors rather than of actors *per se*' (Qin 2016: 43). The assumption is that the international society is a domain populated by diverse sets of actors with disparate interests. Relationality in this setting belies

> a process of negotiating socio-political arrangements that manage complex relationships in a community to produce order so that members behave in a reciprocal and cooperative manner with mutual trust evolved over a shared understanding of social norms and human morality.
>
> (Qin 2016: 43)

Nevertheless, the gist of Qin's logic of relationality is still inherently actor-centric and depends on their dispositions to otherness. As he notes, 'a social actor bases her actions on relations. In other words, the logic holds that *an actor makes judgements and decisions according to her relationships to specific others*' (Qin 2017: 7; emphasis added). What this means is that it is actors rather than relations that select.

Qin's relational governmentality of international interactions has three elements: *inclusivity*, *complementarity*, and *harmony*. *Inclusivity* here refers to the dynamics of mutual constitution of self and other. They are neither detached nor independent of one another, but 'both-and' – that is, the world stage is not populated by impermeable and 'inassimilatable' others, but the identity and practices of each actor contain 'elements of the other though they differ or even though they seem as opposite to each other in their attributes' (Qin 2016: 40). This take on inclusivity informs a relational framing of identity and refuses (as well as refutes) the dichotomous accounts of subjectivity informing the mainstream. Such a relational understanding then shifts the focus away from the containment and/or elimination of difference towards an emphasis on the 'mutual complementation' of differences (Qin 2016: 40). The point here is that *complementarity* disrupts the insistence of Hegelian dialectics that conflict is a 'natural' and necessary feature of world affairs and the framing condition of international interactions. Although differences indeed can lead to confrontation, relationality acts as a reminder that differences are the constitutive preconditions for both coexistence and co-evolution, 'without mutual negation and elimination between opposites' (Qin 2016: 41). Thus, instead of anarchy, *harmony* becomes 'the state of nature and the universal principle of order' (Qin 2016: 41).[8] Harmony here does not imply symmetry of actors, nor does it suggest assimilation into a homogeneous whole. Differences and diversity are the bread and butter of harmonious relations; opposites interact in

> an immanently inclusive way, depending [on] and complementing each other for full expression and for life, and co-evolving into a new synthesis through dynamic processes which keep on maintaining, adjusting, and managing complex and fluid human relations so as to reach the ideal state of harmony.
>
> (Qin 2016: 41)

Zhao Tingyang and the methodological relationalism of Tianxia

A major aspect of current discussions on the Chinese characteristics of IR seems to be the concentration on the notion and practices of *Tianxia* (天下, usually translated as 'all-under-heaven'). As some insist, Tianxia represents 'a total system for the conduct of *all* international relations' (Mancall 1984: 20; emphasis in original). At the same time, it stands for 'a new global imagination that is oriented to cultivating shared values of peace, respect, democracy, and justice among nations and cultures' (Liu 2014: 120). The bulk of these conversations debates the relevance of historical narratives for the explanation and understanding of contemporary world politics. In this respect, many see *Tianxia* as a re-embodiment of *Pax Sinica* – that is, an ambitious strategy for regional and/or global domination through the establishment of a Sinocentric (regional/world) order. Others dismiss such a reading of the *Tianxia* system as a product of Western anxiety produced by unease about the implications from the so-called 'global shift to the East' spearheaded by a rising (and increasingly more confident) China. In other words, the negative depiction of Tianxia reflects a Western strategy (as well as hypocrisy) of narrativizing historical experience by conjuring up images and projections of thinly veiled quasi-imperialistic visions for regional and/ or global governance.

According to the proponents of this position, a more pragmatic and less fearful reading of *Tianxia* might reveal that it functions as a foundational myth not that dissimilar to that of Westphalia in the Euro-centric IR tradition. *Tianxia* thereby makes available a metaphysical pre-scription for the organization of global life.

Probably the most prominent proponent of this view is Zhao Tingyang (赵汀阳). His point of departure is the emphasis on a 'Chinese ontology, the ontology of relations, instead of the Western ontology of things' (Zhao 2006: 33). Such a premise then leads Zhao (2015) to assert that the key dif-ference between the *Tianxia* system and the Westphalian system boils down to the distinction between 'world politics' and 'international politics' – in other words, by pivoting on the 'polis [the Westphalian system] developed inter-state politics, while all-under-heaven invented world politics'. For Zhao, this is a unique framing not merely because of its conceptualization 'in the early days of human civilization', but mostly because it discloses a distinctly '*Chinese*' way of thinking about and engaging in world affairs. Zhao insists that such idiosyncrasy draws on the distinct etymology of the Chinese word for politics which meant,

'justified order' and indicates that the civilized order determines the common fortune of all peoples. It defines a political concept not oppo-site but alternative to politics as the public life of the Greek polis. [Thus], even before Confucius, in the minds of the kings of the all-under-heaven system, the greatest and ultimate goal [of politics] was 'to create harmony of all nations and of all peoples'.

(Zhao 2015: 46)

At the same time, *Tianxia* is 'an open concept' which can continuously 'be renewed or updated by better ideas' (Zhao 2015: 63). Again, looking back at the etymology of the term, Zhao outlines that *Tianxia* reflects the cohabitation of three designations: (1) the physical world – that is, a con-sideration for the whole planet; (2) the psychological world – that is, an affective orientation towards the 'hearts of all peoples' (民心); and (3) the political world – that is, 'a world institution, or a universal system for the world, a utopia of the world-as-one-family' (Zhao 2006: 30–31). In this respect, its revival in political discourse should not be misunderstood as an attempt to return to 'an old pattern that is no longer suitable in the con-temporary context' (Zhao 2015: 64). Equally significantly, any possible future reincarnation of the all-under-heaven system 'does not necessarily mean "a Chinese system", but instead suggests a universal system of and for all' (Zhao 2015: 64).[9] In other words, 'the conceptually defined Empire of All-under-Heaven does not mean a country at all but an institutional world instead' (Zhao 2006: 30).

Tianxia's alleged emphasis on world politics rather than international politics leads Zhao Tingyang to assert that the ideal type of the all-under-heaven proposes a viable relational framework for the study and practice of world politics. For him, *Tianxia* furnishes a relational ordering principle prioritizing the most beneficial mutual interactions (the minimization of mutual harm) rather than the most beneficial unilateral strategy (the maximization of individual interest) (Zhang 2015: 24). Thus, in contrast to the conflictual interactions between the self and its others (invariably framed in Eurocentric IR either as suspicious or as outright enemies), the all-under-heaven system 'proposes politics of harmony for a world in which relations prevail far and near among nations, as opposed to hostile differentiation between self and others. In a world with no enemies, or hostis, harmony becomes possible' (Zhao 2009: 14).

Zhao's suggestion is that Confucianism (and all Chinese philosophical traditions more broadly conceived) offers an alternative framework of explanation and understanding rooted in relations rather than the capacity of individual actors.[10] As he puts it, 'relations, and not *essence* [which for him is a stand-in for Anglophone preoccupations with the identity, subjectivity, and/or individuality of international actors] define what something is' (Zhao 2009: 10; emphasis in original). At the same time, Zhao also makes a distinction between Western preoccupation with rational action and Chinese attention to the effects of interaction:

> The truth is that there is no necessary transition from the mutual understanding of minds to the mutual acceptance of hearts. We also need to be aware that the problem of the other is actually a problem of other hearts rather than other minds, since hearts are not open to concession.
> (Zhao 2009: 19)

According to Zhao, this is the main reason for the failure of most post–World War II attempts at conflict resolution through international organizations. By assuming that international actors are rational opportunity maximizers, such endeavours subscribe to an atomistic view of international agency premised on an ontology of separation that completely disregards the bearing of emotions.

In order to rectify this trend, Zhao proffers 'methodological relationalism' as a cure. Methodological relationalism volunteers a 'universal approach to understanding, analysing, and explaining human actions and values in terms of *relations* rather than *individuals* (independent agents, subjects, or monads)' (Zhao 2015: 49; emphasis in original). In other words, this is an approach that advocates an inclusive global outlook 'through the world' rather than 'of the world', which shows predilection for perspectives only from a certain part of the world (Zhao 2009: 6–8). At the same time, methodological relationalism has a normative slant, as it insists on providing 'a better horizon to discover solutions to the problems of conflict, as well as a more reasonable and feasible approach to deal with problematic situations of the multiversal world and or the multicultural society with peoples of different hearts' (Zhao 2015: 49).

In this setting, Zhao reads the *Tianxia* system as an instance of a relational world politics premised on harmonious interactions embedded in 'family-ship' (Zhao 2015: 49). Consequently, according to 'the ideal of all-under-heaven, the world should be recognized and reconstructed into a universal political system of family-ship (家庭方式/家庭性) so as to minimise conflicts in economics and cultures' (Zhao 2015: 51). Family-ship is construed to be 'the naturally given ground and resource for love, harmony and obligations, and thus a full argument that "exhausts the essence of humanity"' (Zhao 2006: 30). In this context, 'obligations come first in the ranking of values', which presages a relational outlook that asserts that 'relations matter more than individuals' (Zhao 2015: 49–50). Such relationality, however, neither condones nor should be misunderstood as insisting on the establishment of 'suppressive discipline, harsh rules, and excessive routine' (Zhao 2015: 49). The evasion of disorder is not synonymous with the suppression of difference; instead, 'all-under-heaven is meant to be of all and for all, and never of and for anybody in particular' (Zhao 2015: 60). Zhao ascertains that, from a relational point of view, 'an independent individual is not a proper object of inquiry, since it does not make any problem by itself' (Zhao 2015: 49).[11] Thus, in a world defined by dynamic and unpredictable 'processes of uncertain possibilities', 'relationology' offers a meaningful framework for the 'positive consideration of human deeds as the power to partly determine situations' (Zhao 2015: 48). In this respect, the notion and practices of Tianxia outline an ontology of coexistence premised on the consideration that

> My existence is made possible and meaningful if and only if I am in coexistence with others. Moreover, all problems of existence, such as conflict and cooperation, war and peace, happiness and misery, have to be resolved by virtue of coexistence. Therefore, *coexistence is prior to existence.*
>
> (Zhao 2015: 50; emphasis in original)

The irruptive dialogicality of Zhao's ontology of coexistence reflects his methodological relationalism. In particular, it echoes the workings of 'relational calculation' (as opposed to rational calculation), whose basic consideration is 'never demand too much; always leave room for the unknown; and, most important, always take others into consideration (briefly, never maximize self-interest)' (Zhao 2015: 50). The first principle of this ontology of coexistence is 'the *priority of human obligations* (*renyi*)' (Zhao 2015: 50; emphasis in original). Zhao's point here is to frame reciprocity as a general ethical principle 'to do to others as a human being ought to do' (Zhao 2015: 50). Thus, the reciprocity of human obligations offers a contingent and, at the same time, profoundly contextual resolution to conflicts. At the same time, by drawing attention to obligations, Zhao indicates that individual interests can be meaningfully realized only relationally – namely, the guidelines for interaction are provided by reciprocity, mutual help, and the minimization of harm. The second principle reflects the structuring of the Chinese political system into 'families, states, and all-under-heaven (*jia-guo-Tianxia*)' (Zhao 2015: 51). According to Zhao, such framing departs significantly from the Eurocentric emphasis on 'individuals, communities, and nation-states', associated with incessant competition, designed to maximize self-interest, and 'never make a concession unless defeated' (Zhao 2015: 51). Thus, *Tianxia*'s logic of relationality emerges as the very antithesis to Westphalia's logic of violence.

Zhao's relational model pivots on universalism which does not expect or argue for uniformity. Instead, it proposes a 'multiverse of compatibility' through interactions (Zhao 2015: 62). Hence, in contrast to Western modalities of cosmopolitanism redolent of imposing universalizing normativity that should 'apply to all individuals', Tianxia offers a set of principles that would 'apply to all relations' (Zhao 2015: 62). The features of this compatible universalism are (1) tolerating different forms of life for others; (2) prioritizing the universal values of relationships over those of individuality; and (3) favouring mutual interest over self-interest (Zhao 2015: 63). Zhao's point is that because of the elision of relationality from its Eurocentric mainstream, IR seems unable to come to terms both with global life and the full complexity of its interactions. Due to its preoccupation with autonomous selves – mostly, nation-states – IR has failed to account how these have emerged and are sustained by relations. In other words, Zhao finds any type of IR which is focused on inter-state relations wanting because 'such projects have essential difficulties in reading the real integrity of the world' (Zhao 2006: 33–39). As a result, the Anglosphere of IR tends to treat global life as a 'non-world' (Zhao 2015: 52).

Conclusion

Rooted in the conviction that global life outlines a domain, space, narrative, and dynamic of 'multiple actors, traditions, and practices' (Katzenstein 2010: 23), the contributions to the relational turn in IR draw attention to the ongoing interpenetration between agency, structure, and order amongst the diversity of agency, form, and mater implicated in, enacting, and enabling global life. The insights from the conversations on relationality thus challenge the conviction that the appropriate way to acquire knowledge about the world is through the modelling of linear relationships with homogeneous independent variables that discern between discrete and stochastic and systemic effects (Earnest 2015; Rosenau 1990).

This chapter offers an overview of some of the key proponents of relationality in IR – both in its Anglophone and Sinophone variants. The first part of the chapter outlined the processual relationalism proffered by Jackson and Nexon and the relational coexistence ushered in by Odysseos as instances of conversations in Anglophone IR. The second part of the chapter discusses the relational theory of world politics proposed by Qin Yaqing and the methodological relationalism of Zhao Tingyang as examples of Sinophone debates. As indicated, such a review does not pretend to be comprehensive or exhaustive and does not do justice to the full spectrum of relational approaches evident in both Anglophone and Sinophone discussions on relationality. The point, however, is that the instances included in this chapter offer a good illustration of the current state of the art on relationality both in the Anglosphere and Sinosphere of IR.

In this setting, Chapter 3 will provide a dialogue between the Anglophone and Sinophone conversations on relationality. Drawing on the concept and practices of *guanxi*, the analysis aims to amplify as well as analyze the intrinsic relationality of global life and the realms of IR. In contrast to the dualistic bifurcations that dominate IR imaginaries, the encounter and engagement with concepts such as *guanxi* both illuminate and remind the study of world affairs that the complex patterns of global life resonate with the fragility, fluidity, and mutuality of global interactions, rather than the static and spatial arrangements implicit in the fetishized currency of self–other/centre–periphery/hegemon–challenger models underpinning the binary metanarratives of IR. This is a major departure from the current state of the art on relationality in IR; rather than looking at dyadic sets of relations as well as the identities and capacity of individual actors, the preceding engagement with *guanxi* inheres an IR pivoted on webs of figurations intertwined by a conscious and strategic search for relations with others. International actors are not just isolated entities moving about in the vacuum of world affairs; instead, they are entangled in and produced by multitudes of relations among and across many different spatio-temporal contexts. In this respect, actors (and their agency) have effects only to the extent that they are *in relation* with others. At the same time, the notion of relationality suggests that the interactions of global life are not just self-organizing and co-constitutive, but that they can hardly be regulated.

Notes

1 Yet in this account, coexistence seems to become a placeholder and a formal indicator of a phenomenon still very much obscured by and very much hemmed in by subjectivist thinking. In spite of her emphasis on relational coexistence, Odysseos' account is still informed by the existence of distinct self and other prior to and independent of the contingent circumstances of international relations. As such, the dynamics of interaction allow the self and other to *see* each and recognize their mutual implication. Although this implies sociality, it does not necessarily equate with relationality. Odysseos' coexistential self is not a relational one. As she puts it, an actor is 'an other-constituted and coexistential being, a being determined through and through by otherness' (Odysseos 2007: xxxiv). A relational self would imply something different altogether – namely, the actuality and possibility of relations. It is the co-constitutive dynamics of interaction and actorness that reveal the transactional capacity to play different roles in the context of circumstantial and contingent interactions. In this respect, it is not so much the subjectivity of the self and other that are reflected in the ontology of relations, but the roles that they play over time with one another. The residue of subjectivist thinking not only thwarts Odysseos' efforts, but also prevents her from looking into the possibility that things happen when actors dwell together. In other words, the static reading of coexistence as 'the condition of staying-together' (Odysseos 2007: 90) obscures its relational implications. The point here is that co-presence is not necessarily only a fixture of stasis; it is also a dynamic practice that opens possibilities for interactive engagement and social experimentation (and entrepreneurship) that have a bearing on the roles through which actors engage in this specific context, each other, and the world. In other words, relationality is also about what actors happen to do together while interactive co-present in the same temporal and spatial context; the practices of this co-dwelling assist with the evolution of dynamic understandings of who they are and how they perceive each other which are entangled in the very social circumstances on which they rest. It is the contingent dynamism of interactions that belies the fundamental relationality of global life.

2 Yet such relational understanding of coexistence is primarily motivated by the recognition of and the transformative possibilities made available by the constitutive role of otherness rather than relations. As Odysseos insists, her optics of coexistence offer an analytical lens through which we can see that 'otherness constitutes [international actors] in multiplicity of ways . . . by always already providing a world of meaning, norms, rules, and practices that help [these actors] orient their existence and everyday interactions' (Odysseos 2007: 82). Such relationality performs a critical role in the objectification of otherness by Eurocentric IR scholarship as something to be observed and known, but

always and only detached from the Western self. Thus, Odysseos' endeavours contribute meaningfully to the repertoire of IR's explanation and understanding by recollecting that knowledge about the world, as well as the world itself, is produced and reproduced socially in the context of ongoing interactions.

3 The limits of her account of relationality are adumbrated by the inability to transgress the self-other binary belying the Eurocentrism of IR. As Odysseos insists, being-in-the-world *with others* entails a relational self which is 'undistinguishable from others', while at the same time existing ' "outside of itself" among the things and being that constitute it' (Odysseos 2007: 59).

4 In fact, in this aspect, Qin almost reiterates the point made by Odysseos (2007: xxiii) that IR takes relations to be self-evident rather than addresses relationality as a question, as an issue that has to be examined, debated, contested. Unfortunately, he does not refer to or engage with her work.

5 Qin, however, seems to overlook that processes themselves have agency; instead, in his account agency seems to be actor-centred.

6 Yet despite such claims, Qin's analysis seems to confuse actors' role and identity: As Qin (2016: 36) states, the distinct feature of Chinese relationality is that 'there is no me in isolation to be considered abstractly: I am the totality of roles I live'. It is this emphasis on roles – and the very practice of distinct and multiple roles – that provides the crux of any Chinese-inspired take on relationality. Such shift away from Western preoccupations with identity/subjectivity/individuality challenges all attempts to offer a Confucian version of either constructivism or the English School (Qin 2009; Uemura 2015; Zhang 2015). In other words, what changes in the process of interaction are the roles that actors play, not their subjectivities and/or identities. Yet rather than elaborate this opening further, Qin slides back into the preoccupation with self–other relations that is the defining feature of Western IR. As he insists, the emergent complexly related whole which is the global universe of interrelatedness 'actors tend to make decisions according to the degrees of intimacy and/or importance of her relationships to specific others, with the totality of her relational circles as the background' (Qin 2016: 37). Thus, rather than a contingent web of ongoing interactions, relationality *de facto* becomes a (distinct, although not that dissimilar from its non-Chinese variants) mode of encounter and engagement with otherness. Thus, what is potentially the most transformative Confucian contribution of Qin's relational theory of IR becomes subsumed into what Odysseos calls the *singularity* of coexistence: ' "singularity never has the nature of individuality. Singularity never takes place at the level of atoms, those identifiable, if not identical identities"; rather, singularity has to do with the inclination or disposition to otherness' (Odysseos 2007: xxxii).

7 This statement also seems to indicate that Qin's version of the logic of relationality still tends to reassert the centrality of actors over relations.

8 Yet if one is to look more carefully Qin's insistence on an instrumental/expressive bifurcation, this can be easily mapped onto the distinction between choice and process proposed by Jackson and Nexon. The point here is that Qin has more in common with the processual relationalism developed by Jackson and Nexon than he is willing to admit.

9 This is an important point aimed at discouraging the anxiety among some Western observers about the imperial designs behind *Tianxia*. As Zhao Tingyang and many others have pointed out, although undergirded by strong normative universalism, its vision of world order is not about global domination. In this

respect, Feng Zhang's prescient analysis of the *Tianxia* system stresses that 'Chinese rulers usually recognized the limits of their own power, and they harboured no intention to rule the entire world. Even the boundaries of an ideologically constructed Sinocentric world – the *tianxia* – varied in different times and even in the mind of the same ruler. But the pretence of universalism was nonetheless strong, and the stated intention was to create with all the peoples of the known world a hierarchical authority relationship in political and familial terms according to emperor-vassal and father-son role differentiation' (Zhang 2016: 158–159).

10 Zhao Tingyang is quite explicit that *Tianxia* is not coterminous with Confucianism, but reflects modes of thought and action preceding, intertwining, and transcending the Confucian oeuvre.

11 Zhao goes on to elaborate that the 'question about the individual is neither meaningful, nor answerable unless it is a question clearly defined in terms of relations with others. In other words, the meaning of a thing consists not in itself, but in its relations with other. When we say a man is selfish, this is a description rather than a question. We question only problematic relations . . . For instance, a man acts rather than simply is. No one is good by himself; one's presence as such is decided by one's relations with others; that is, a man is good only in so far as he acts to someone with goodness' (Zhao 2015: 49).

3   The *guanxi* of relationality

Introduction

How China thinks and in what ways its history and traditions inform the idiosyncrasies of China's international outlook have grown into a cottage industry, both in IR and across the full spectrum of the humanities and social sciences. As Benjamin Schwartz (1967: 92) presciently observed 50 years ago, the issue which always seems to stump China is whether ' "the Chinese" [are] prepared to accept the nation-state system that governs the international life of the West or are their images of the world and of China's place in it still governed by cultural habits derived from the remote past'? On the one hand, such concern reflects IR's tendency to organize around the perceived experiences, interests, and concerns of powerful (Western) nation-states (Chowdhry and Rai 2009: 85). On the other hand, at the heart of this query is China's positioning in European intellectual imagination as the ultimate Other, or what Michel Foucault ([1973] 2002) called *heterotopia* – a disturbing place, whose difference 'undermines language'. China becomes 'the Other country' not merely because of its location on the opposite end of the Eurasian landmass, but also because it represents 'a culture entirely devoted to the ordering of space, but one that does not distribute the multiplicity of existing things into any of the categories that make it possible for us to name, speak, and think' (Foucault [1973] 2002: xix).[1]

In this setting, China's rise appears not only to question 'the very "constitutional structures" ' of IR's explanation and understanding (Carlson 2010: 96), but also calls on IR theory to break free from its Columbus syndrome by going back to the road less travelled of encountering the multiverse of relations animating global life. Writing in the context of a world order defined by the arrangements of the Congress of Vienna, the American legal reformer David Dudley Field considered the conceptualization of China's position in international affairs. Seemingly puzzled, he queried:

> Can it be justly claimed that a nation which has maintained a regularly administered government over hundreds of millions of human beings

for thousands of years . . . is uncivilized? It must be admitted, I think that the point of civilization is not the one on which the question of international law, in its application to China, should turn.

(Field 1884: 452–453)

Thus, the debates on whether China is going to comply with established (Western) standards of international behavior or adopt a conflictual stance reveal that 'international law [is still] regarded as a tool owned and used by the West to exploit the rest, including China' (Chan 1999: 175). Although more nuanced than the racialized sensibilities of its nineteenth-century modality, the Columbus syndrome still informs the perceptions and sensibility of Anglophone IR of Beijing's global agency.

This chapter therefore intends an interpretative theoretical journey into the Chinese concepts and definitions of the international with the intention to explore whether they indeed are so heterotopic as to be unworthy of translation (let alone threatening) for IR theory building. It has to be stated at the outset that the focus on *guanxi* (traditional: 關係 simplified: 关系) is not entirely coincidental. It is one of the words that make up the Chinese term for 'international relations' – *guoji guanxi* (traditional: 國際 關係 simplified: 国际关系). In this respect, it should appear surprising that there has been so little attention to the meaning and content of the terms that go into the making of the Chinese phrase for IR. What is particularly telling is that one does not have to be fluent in Chinese to encounter the complex texture of the term – for instance, the cognate literatures on cultural studies, cross-cultural communication, psychology, and sociology (to name only a few) offer a huge repository of information about the meaning and practices of *guanxi*. The first part of this chapter draws on these literatures to tease out the content and practices of this term, as well as its implications for IR theory and practice. The attention is to the ways in which the affordances of relationality are foreshadowed or foreshortened by the engagement with the concept of *guanxi*. The second part of the chapter points to some of the ways in which the concept of *guanxi* informs nascent modes of relational theorizing in IR.

Such an endeavour also probes the possibilities for dialogue between the Anglophone and Sinophone takes on relationality outlined in the preceding Chapter 2. In particular, the aim is to suggest how both the relational turn and IR theory would look if they were to be imagined with the help of the concept and practices of *guanxi*. As already outlined in the introductory chapter to this book, the necessary caveat is that *guanxi* is deployed here as a heuristic device revealing the infinite capacity of (international) interactions to create and construct multiple worlds rather than as a term illustrating the actual practices of Chinese foreign policy.[2] Although such connections are clearly there (especially in places like Central Asia and in initiatives such as the 'One Belt, One Road' policy), the point here is to disclose an epistemically and ontologically relational theory of IR made possible by the encounter with *guanxi*. In other words, the following sections do not discuss the international practices of China, but the ways in which Chinese (and by extension other non-Western) concepts – such as *guanxi* – can aid the disclosure of alternative and, especially, relational modes of IR theorizing. The proposition is that the irruptive translation of such relational IR theory building resonates with the emancipatory mutuality of many different ways of knowing and being in global life that promise a politics for 'a more just coexistence of worlds' (Rojas 2016: 370).

Guanxi: what's in a name?

Perhaps one of the most memorable images from the diplomatic rapprochement between the United States and the People's Republic of China during the 1970s was the opulent banquet that President Richard Nixon and Premier Zhou Enlai shared at the Great Hall of the People. In front of the whirring cameras of international media one of the most important realignments of the Cold War period was taking place around a table brimming with Chinese culinary delights dished out for the Americans by their Chinese hosts. As the food historian Andrew Coe insists, Chairman Mao had personally instructed Zhou Enlai to restore connections with the non-communist world by wining and dining foreign leaders (Coe 2009). At the banquet in the Great Hall of the People, Premier Zhou presented Nixon with a bottle of *moutai* (distilled Chinese liquor) which he had kept for over 30 years, while Mao personally added a dish of *hongshao huashi* (a soy sauce–braised herring tail) to the lunch the two had on the previous day.[3] It seems therefore that in order to end the country's self-imposed isolation, the Chinese leader was resorting to an age-old practice embedded in the traditions that his cultural revolution intended to eradicate – namely, *guanxi*.

Although several recent IR studies have made reference to the term *guanxi* (Huang and Shih 2014; Jørgensen and Wong 2016; Kavalski 2012; 2016; Pan 2016; Uemura 2015; Wong 2013), none of them have engaged its complex history and etymology. It is therefore necessary to offer a brief account of the meanings that this term has come to acquire before outlining its contributions to IR thinking. To begin with *guanxi* appears to be one of those essentially contested concepts whose meaning and practices are anything but clear-cut and universally accepted (Hwang 1987: 963; Jia 2006: 49–54; Luo 1997: 49).[4] Almost all commentators acknowledge the Confucian underpinnings of such practices, although many also assert that *guanxi* has become shorthand for patterns of thought and behaviour predating the time and teachings of Confucius. Rather than a constraining straitjacket, such intellectual legacy seems to have provided an enabling platform for contingent innovation – after all, Confucius himself acknowledged the entrepreneurial endeavour of his efforts by calling himself a 'co-worker with antiquity' (Ford 2010: 17). Such an entrepreneurial move becomes part and parcel of the nascent 'creative transformation of Chinese tradition' (Lin Yusheng quoted in Liu 2014: 121).

More often than not, *guanxi* is understood to denote the establishment and maintenance of 'an intricate and pervasive relational network' engendered by the practice of unlimited exchange of favours between its members and bound by reciprocal obligation, assurance, and mutuality (Luo 1997: 44; Alston 1989: 28; Pye 1982: 882). In this setting, banquet giving – as both Henry Kissinger and Nixon discovered in the early 1970s – performs a crucial role in engendering and sustaining positive sentiments among participants, who might initially be inimical to one another. Although not unique to Chinese culture, the practices of food sharing play a distinct role in informalizing interactions – especially in transforming diplomatic relations into interpersonal ones and drawing foreign representatives into establishing friendship ties which then make them subject to the 'blandishments and pressures of the Chinese social order' (Walker 2012: 495; Solomon 1995: 9). This seems to confirm Lucian Pye's insistence that Chinese politics (both domestic and international) 'rest on the bonding powers of personal relationships [owing to] the very pragmatic, utilitarian function of *guanxi*' (Pye 1995: 53). In this respect, Richard H. Solomon observed at the time that 'as the common [Chinese] saying goes, if you eat the things of others you will find it difficult to raise your hand against them' (Solomon (1975: 53). And, indeed, the practice of food sharing – especially, the opulent Peking duck dinners that Kissinger and Zhou Enlai shared during their secret negotiations in the run-up to the Mao–Nixon meeting – appears to have played an important role in lubricating the Sino-American relationship. While the American diplomats commented (and commended) the sophistication and deftness with which Zhou Enlai was introducing and serving the various dishes, such meals both mellowed the tensions and allowed the two sides to begin changing their preconceptions about one another (Coe 2009: 228–230). The record of these diplomatic banquets illustrates the key underlying feature of this kind of interaction either in interpersonal or international relations – namely, 'to provide a friendly feeling . . . and unless it did this it failed its purpose' (Sahlins 1972: 220).

Although *guanxi* has been labelled 'the lifeblood of all things Chinese – business, politics, and society' (Luo 1997: 45), 'one of the most fundamental aspects of Chinese political behaviour' (Pye 1995: 35), the 'key to the Chinese way of thinking' (Pan 2016: 305), and a central philosophical concept that 'reflects the Chinese way to know about reality (ontology), the Chinese way to interpret reality (phenomenology), and the Chinese values about humanity (axiology)' (Jia 2006: 49–54), its widespread usage appears to be of very recent provenance.[5] In particular, *guanxi*'s rise to prominence seems to be closely associated with social, political, and economic processes set in motion during the second half of the twentieth century across the 'Chinese commonwealth' – in mainland China, Taiwan, Hong Kong, Macau, and Singapore, as well as the Sinophonic diaspora around the globe (Gold et al. 2002: 13–14; Luo 1997: 44; Langenberg 2007: 4; Yeung and Tung 1996: 58). In this setting, *guanxi* has acquired positive connotations (associated with bottom-up empowerment) and negative flavours (associated with graft).[6] Both of these connotations of *guanxi* draw on shared resources and capacities. In particular, *guanxi* ties seem to (1) arise from the propensity of their practices to subvert established structures of authority; (2) reflect an idiosyncratic encounter between tradition and modernity in the socio-political and economic development of the state; and (3) become support networks in times of need (Kipnis 1997; Ledeneva 2008; Yang 2002).[7]

Probably the central Confucian inflection of *guanxi* is the deontological commitment to act in accordance with social demands and expectations.[8] It needs to be reiterated that these commitments are not constraining, nor do they deny spontaneity and improvisation; instead, they merely reflect the dependence on and persistence of relationships – both of which entail a 'responsibility to *respond* to the reactions of and needs of others' (Weakland 1950: 365; emphasis in original). Thus, as some have pointed out,

> [i]f the Greek conception of political community is *political* or *collective*, then the Chinese conception can be called *ethical*. In the Chinese conception, the importance of politics lies not in collective participation in collective decisions but in its promotion of the highest moral good in individual lives (*ren*), and its accompanying moral order.
>
> (Chan 2008: 70; emphasis in original)

In other words, the patterns, practices, experiences, and frameworks of *guanxi* undergird 'one of the most significant features of Chinese culture' – namely, the continuous maintenance of a 'harmonious society' alongside the ongoing management of 'the appropriate arrangement of interpersonal relations' (Abbott 1970: 181; Hwang 1987: 944). In their Confucian framing, *guanxi* practices are embedded in the four virtues (benevolence [*ren*], appropriateness [*yi*], propriety [*li*], and wisdom [*zhi*]) and emphasize reciprocal obligations framed by five cardinal social role relations (*wu-lun*): (1) ruler–subject; (2) father–son; (3) husband–wife; (4) older brother–younger brother; (5) elder friend–junior friend (Tu 1985: 162). Framed by metaphors of kinship, each of these roles comes with certain duties that each side needs to enact faithfully in their relations.[9] If those obligations are not fulfilled – that is, if favours done are not reciprocated – the reputation of the transgressor is tarnished.[10] Thus, the implicit threat of social sanctions is often sufficient to ensure that favours are repaid, that obligations are met, and that relationships are honoured.

It is important to note that in a Confucian context even though *guanxi* relations are asymmetrical, they are nevertheless volitional – in other words, the structure of hierarchy should not be misunderstood as giving one side influence over the other. On the contrary, the very nature of reciprocal obligation belies its constraining power on both sides of the *guanxi* tie (Barbalet 2015: 1046).[11] In particular, the interdependence, mutuality, and reciprocity characterizing *guanxi* accords social relations much greater significance, and relations are often seen as ends in and of themselves rather than means for realizing various individual goals. Thus, although

> norms of reciprocity (*bao*) are intense, these norms are heavily shaped by the hierarchically structured network of social relations (*guanxi*) in which people are embedded by the public nature of obligations, and by the long time period over which obligations are incurred through a self-conscious manipulation of face and related symbols [such as reputation].
>
> (Hwang 1987: 944)

According to Lucian Pye, this pattern is at the heart of what he sees as the key paradox of *guanxi*:

> It [China] has had a vision of politics that operates without the open articulation of interests. Instead, in China the functions which legal norms perform in administration and which interests serve for politics in most political systems have been largely met in China by the extraordinary powers of *guanxi*. This substitution has been possible because for most Chinese the structuring of human relationships has such a vivid quality as to be a very substantive part of physical reality. In practice, *guanxi* in action has thus structured authority and given order and form to Chinese governance and to what passes as both administration and politics. It has been particularism in the service of generalized institution-building – which helps explain why Chinese public life can be so orderly without being institutionalized ... The particularistic basis of a relationship does not in itself provide a clear clue for predicting the purposes for which the relationship might be directed. Parties might be associated with each other, for example, because they came

from the same town or province, but this would almost never mean that they would therefore work together for the interests of that place. In short, the particularistic basis of the relationship is not a guide as to what it may be applied towards. Indeed, *the very power of* guanxi *is that its workings are not limited to its ostensible basis but rather it can be universally directed and used for multiple and diverse purposes.*

(Pye 1995: 43–44; emphasis added)

A central feature of *guanxi*'s network of reciprocal obligation is the claim that

the self so conceived is not a static structure but a dynamic process. It is a *center* of relationships, not an enclosed world of private thoughts and feelings. It needs to reach out, to be in touch with other selves, and to communicate through an ever-expanding network of human relatedness.

(Tu 1985: 133)[12]

The key inference is that participants in a *guanxi* perceive each other to be 'role occupants rather than individuals' (Hwang 1987: 945).[13] This assumption challenges all attempts to offer a Confucian version of either constructivism (Qin 2009; 2016; Uemura 2015) or the English School (Zhang 2015, 2016). In other words, what changes in the process of interaction are the roles that actors play, not their identity, subjectivity, and/or individuality. This should not be misunderstood as a suggestion that the identities, subjectivities, and/or individualities of international actors (in contrast to their roles) remain immutable or are unaffected by the occurrence(s) of interaction. On the contrary, the point here is that by focusing on identities, IR analyses tend to reify misleading representational modes for explanation and understanding that freeze the flow of international interactions into static relationships that actors *have*, 'as if they were those self-same, permanent objects whose interactions with the world produce external circumstantial changes to the objects' (Kavalski 2018a). In the context of ongoing dynamic change, actors *are* their relationships. Roles therefore are not about identities (nor are they prescribed by them), but about acting on the world stage – an actor can play any role depending on the circumstances.[14]

In this setting, it is useful to remind ourselves that

Deng Xiaoping was never constrained in his career by any job description of his posts [i.e., the power resources made available to him through his professional identity]. He was much too active in building relationships [i.e., *guanxi* – open himself to ties that would allow him to play different roles in multiple spheres of relations].

(Pye 1995: 38)

Likewise, Lee Kuan Yew, often referred to as the founding father of modern Singapore, has acknowledged that the Chinese use *guanxi* 'to make up for the lack of rule of law and transparency in rules and regulation' (cited in Yeung and Tung 1996: 56). These statements intuit that, in practical terms, *guanxi* (and the networks that its patterns sustain) acts as a substitute for an institutional structure (enabling participants to acquire needed resources, information, and other support) (Farh et al. 1998: 480). In this respect, the focus on *guanxi* might suggest that China's international interactions are far more institutionalized than current paradigms (both in the Anglosphere and Sinosphere of IR) are willing to admit.

Thus (and *contra* Wendtian forms of constructivism), rather than endogenous, roles are exogenous to actors and emerge in relation to the context of interaction and change over time and space. In fact, the very idea of intentionality itself 'cannot be removed from the context in which it arises' (Wen and Wang 2013: 187). Role demands, therefore, never emerge in the abstract nor are they pre-given, but are borne out of the very processes of interaction. Depending on the interactive circumstances, an actor can be accommodative and generous (as China seems to be in its interactions with African countries, for instance) and assertive and vengeful (as China seems to act in the South China Sea), *all at the same time*. The role-centric framing of *guanxi* underpins not only its malleability (i.e., that it can be used for multiple and diverse purposes), but its potential to engender resilient connections in the context of recognizing and influencing emergent opportunities. Due to the fluid ways in which these relational roles are lived, *guanxi* asserts that change rather than stability is an endemic feature of global life.

Both through attrition and accretion and depending on the circumstances, issues, and situations, the *guanxi* relationship has diverse and contingent iterations which demand ongoing re-examination and adaptations from all those involved in its webs of reciprocal implication. In short, different social contexts produce different arrangements of relationality. Instancing such development are China's practices of 'plurilateral regionalism' (such as the Shanghai Cooperation Organization [SCO]), 'plurilateral embedded orders' (such as support for the Chiang Mai Initiative Multilateralization), 'plurilateral parallel orders' (such as the Asian Infrastructure Investment Bank), and network governance (such as the OBOR policy).[15] Such pattern also seems to conform with the historical trajectories of Chinese strategic culture, where the structure of world order was always conceived of relationally in terms of the emperor's distinct bilateral relationships [i.e., *guanxi* ties] with his subjects, inside and outside the empire, rather than in the interstate terms that have come to dominate modern international relations.

(Zhang 2016: 159)

Such dynamic multiplicity of interdependent conditioning factors engenders an interpersonal realm whose complexity is only partially known to the participating actors. This outlook calls for a contextual attunement to the transient constellations of factors and actors that affect the content, trajectories, and possible transformations in any social relationship – regardless of whether they occur on an interpersonal, regional, or global level. In particular, the long-term orientation of *guanxi* inserts a modicum of predictability by lowering the transaction costs and ensuring the peaceful resolution of conflicts.[16] The underlying aim is to aid the ability to engage an ever-changing world.

What can we *guanxi* about in international relations?

What would a relational theory of IR claim if we were to imagine it with the help of *guanxi*? The obvious response to such a query is the assertion that IR is about the arrangement and management of *guanxi* rather than the mobilization and manipulation of power. At the same time, the concept and practices of *guanxi* not merely 'reimagine the global', but also assist IR to encounter a world of constant and ongoing co-constitution and co-construction (Liu 2014: 130). At the same time, the outline of such an endeavour should not appear particularly outlandish (let alone heterotopic) to those attuned to the inescapable condition of mutual encounter defining global life (Coles 2016: 25; Kavalski 2016: 559). The reference to relationality is not merely a stand-in for thriving on relationships. The relationality uncovered by the practices of *guanxi* reflects a condition of intelligibility for the sense-making processes on the world stage. Thus, due to prior conditions of relationality, an 'international' world of holistically structured meaning appears in the first place. In this setting, the various actors that animate global life can be articulated, encountered, and accounted for because they are (always) already relationally structured (Kompridis 2006: 32–33). The decentring implicit in such an engagement draws attention to the idiosyncratic structural conditions and unique cultural categories that contribute to the participants' thinking about and involvement in interpersonal situations (Hwang 1987: 946). The contention here is that the encounter with the notion of *guanxi* evinces *relational IR theorizing* as *an optics which both acknowledges the agency of 'others' and through which meanings are generated contingently through interactions in communities of practice, whose relations are premised on the variable reputations of participants and the necessity for ongoing reiteration of the commitment to do things together.* The following paragraphs offer a preliminary unpacking of some of the ways in which the concept of *guanxi* informs such relational IR theorizing.

Guanxi implies both a propensity and a capacity for living *with* and *in* ambiguity. In this respect, as already indicated in Chapter 2, *guanxi* ties provide a 'relational' (as opposed to 'rule-based') framework for the meaningful contextualization in the shifting patterns of global life (Qin 2011). What passes for world affairs in such a context is not about 'the application of abstract norms to cases', but about 'a set of particular international relationships, with concrete obligations defined within the context of each relationship' (Womack 2008: 265). What this means is that rules do not function as such outside of the relationships in which they emerge. In this respect, it is the interaction context that matters rather than the rules themselves. Patterns of order and their social environment *stand in relation of reciprocal influence* (Gottlieb 1983: 593). As Qin Yaqing demonstrates, this understanding reframes power away from its association with the material possession of capacities for influence (regardless of whether they are coercive or not), and instead as a 'relational practice' (Qin 2009: 9). This then becomes the centrepiece for a 'logic of relationships' animating global life (Kavalski 2013; Shih 2016; Womack 2008).[17] Such a logic assumes that

> while the future is unknown, the partners in the future are the same as in the past and present. Therefore, the bottom line is that both sides feel that they are better off if the relationship continues – this is the minimum meaning of 'mutual benefit. A normal relationship does not require symmetry of partners or equality of exchanges, but it does require reciprocity [i.e., respect for the other].
>
> (Womack 2008: 295–297)

This is where the symbolic role of gift giving (within the communications frameworks of *guanxi*) assists both with establishing relations and with binding participants in shared practices.

Such respect for the other inheres not only the possibility of increasing interaction, negotiation, and active contribution to the dynamics, definition, and development of global life, but also the very power to participate, interact, and engage (Kavalski 2016). It should be stated at the outset that such framing should not be misunderstood as an indication of a selfless outlook on global life, but as an effective strategy for managing a hyper-social environment. The logic of relationships outlines a context for action in which goals can be achieved through an active, committed, and responsible involvement in world affairs that takes into account both the broader context of international interactions and the specificities of a particular interactive environment (regardless of whether it is bilateral or multilateral). This demands both contextual sensitivity and an ongoing commitment to the deliberate practices of relationality from all sides involved in the interaction. Unsurprisingly, therefore, a key feature of *guanxi*'s dynamic outlook is the emphasis on harmony (Nordin 2015, 2016). Zhao Tingyang explains the idealization of harmony as a historically informed cultural practice for dealing with conflicts:

> The world is understood as an always open story of unpredictable changes in forms of order and disorder, a story of neither linear progress to the end of history, nor the determined cycle of fatalism. In other words, the world exists as a process of uncertain possibilities. [Thus] neither war nor peace is the best solution to the problem of conflicts ... Beyond the concepts of war and peace, 'harmony' seeks to offer reasonable resolutions of conflicts and stable security by building truly reliable correlations of mutual benefit in the long run, as well as *reciprocal acceptance of the other's values.*
>
> (Zhao 2015: 48; emphasis added)

In short, the principle of 'seeking the common while preserving differences' bespeaks a 'dialogical universalism' of 'harmony without homogeneity' (Liu 2014: 133). In such a relational framing, the notion of harmony denotes neither a fixed state nor a permanent condition; instead, it infers an ongoing and dynamic process beckoning 'appropriate interrelations with the world' (Shen 1994: 172; Wen and Wang 2013: 193).[18] Thus, just like the metaphor of anarchy backstops a self-help international system prioritizing material capabilities, the narratives of harmony outline a pattern of order premised on reciprocal relationships which pays a premium for the dedicated cultivation of connectivity in the context of an ongoing demonstration of respect for the other. The point here is that *guanxi* ties are volitional – actors intentionally commit to the interaction by demonstrating their willingness to exercise self-restraint. Such *guanxi* dynamics should not be misunderstood as altruism; on the contrary, they are pointedly strategic – for instance, China's global outreach can be read as a policy of preemptive interaction intent on allaying the concerns of other international actors and motivated by 'the hope for better future gain or less future loss by preserving positive relations with all concerned parties' (Huang and Shih 2014: 20). However, the role of ethics underpinning the logic of harmonious international interactions reveals that notions such as reciprocity and interdependence are undergirded by 'the assumption that if your neighbour does better, you do better' – thus offering 'a productive framework within which a community of nations can work towards negotiating a common good' (Ames 2011: 265).

In such a relational setting, agency (especially international agency) is not about the intentional projection of self-interest, but about strategic receptivity – that is, 'knowing oneself insofar as one is related to others, and knowing others insofar as others are related to oneself' (Wen and Wang 2013: 192).[19] It is a messy and unpredictable social process framed in the context of interacting with others. Rather than impeding the policy process, such contextual embeddedness discloses the unexpected opportunities made possible by the pattern of *guanxi* – for instance, as evidenced by the unintended evolution of the Shanghai-5 into the 'One Belt, One Road' initiative via the Shanghai Cooperation Organization.[20] The inference here is that international agency emerges in a community, not in a vacuum; in particular, in the relational web of interdependent coexistence, such actorness emerges as

> 'a complex event rather than a discrete thing', a process of 'becoming' rather than an essential 'being', an on-going 'doing' rather than an autonomous 'is', a configuration of concrete, dynamic, and constitutive relations rather than an individuated substance defined by some subsisting agency.
>
> (Ames 2011: 213)

In particular, it is communities of practice that locate *guanxi*'s logic of relationships. The animating force of such relationality appears to be a commitment to the practice of doing things together, which affords ongoing opportunities for interpretative articulation and re-articulation of international exchanges that can engender, enhance, and reaffirm the reputational profile of participating actors – an aspect that can explain China's general aversion to the imposition of conditionality on its partners.

The rationale here seems to be that because rules are defined in the context of interaction, maintaining the relationship offers a viable solution to resolving the problem of new meaning generation. In short, 'there will always be emergent rules. We just need to figure them out' (Hammond and Glenn 2004: 30), and communities of practice tend to offer the most meaningful way for such an undertaking. In particular, communities of practice offer a dynamic understanding of appropriateness whose meaning and practice change over time and space. The point here is that such relationships are not motivated by self-interest, but by the practice of doing things together; at the same time, these are mutual, deeply affective, and even inextricable

(Gottlieb 1983: 595). As it was already mentioned in this chapter, such relational practice does not deny the strategic and/or pragmatic character of interactions, but only that they are not egotistical (and individualistic) in the Eurocentric sense of this term. It is the environment of relational dialogues – as opposed to dominance or interpersonal influence – that allows participants to engage in interactions that can lead to meaningful (yet always and already contextual) knowledge and meaning creation (Abell and Simmons 2000). The accent is on the strategic value of maintaining the relationship rather than on the pursuit of immediate gains. In this respect, the interactive dynamics of communities of practice stimulate new and contextual definitions of the 'common good' by drawing attention to the distinct roles and positions that international actors take in diverse spatial and temporal contexts.[21] In this process, communities of practice reveal a new way of being present in the world through the binding power (as well as social energy) of deliberate interactions.

Thus, as the hub of social knowledge and social life, the patterns of *guanxi* intimate that shared understandings are not imposed as rules, rights, or obligations, but emerge *in, from,* and *through* the very process of interaction. In other words, norms, privileges, claims, immunities, expectations, obligations, and responsibilities are all relationship based and role dependent (Tan and Snell 2002: 362). *Guanxi* thereby presages an understanding of international action and agency – both cognitively and affectively – as simultaneously shaped and mediated by ethical obligations and commitments to others (the structure and content of which are acquired through the very relationships by which ethical obligations and commitments to others are disclosed). At the same time, the context provided by communities of practice rearticulates agency as a 'reflexive response' (Cha 1982: 11) compelled by the demands made by the other participants in the interaction. The patterns of relationality reveal a framework of social interactions binding participants together by a variety of expectations, interests, activities, enterprises, or vulnerabilities in an ongoing and durable way (Gottlieb 1983: 595). The 'long-term balance sheet' of *guanxi* requires skills for living (if not thriving) in a social environment beyond the control of any of the participating actors (Luo 1997). Such relationality is not zero-sum – that is, 'the debit and credit sides of this [relational] balance sheet are never in equilibrium' – because this would spell the end of *guanxi* (Yeung and Tung 1996: 20). What is important emerges not as a result of individual decisions, but relationally in the process of interactions with others and becomes meaningful in the context of doing things together with them.

The currency of such relationality is not legitimacy (as most IR scholars seem to suggest), but reputation. As will be explained in the conclusion of this book, reputation (especially the position of authority) is premised on recognition – one that emerges in the context of interactions and requires ongoing reiteration. The cultivation of reputation (a feature which IR observers tend to subsume within analyses of status) is probably the key aspiration of *guanxi*. As Jack Barbalet cogently observes, reputational standing is a social and not an economic resource. Thus, *guanxi* is deployed not with the aim to gain access to economic or political resources, but is 'primarily directed to acquiring and expending social resources' (Barbalet 2015: 1044). Not only that, but such understanding of relationality demands that those engaged in interactions are 'more aware of the relationships that constitute the objects of their concern than they are of their own interests' (Barbalet 2013: 346).[22] In this respect, *guanxi* becomes a setting for relational 'impression management' – that is, the entanglement in interactions 'to shape and instil in the minds of others [a] particular[ly] favourable image' by demonstrating capacity to act in accordance with social demands and obligations (Hwang 1987: 960). Thus, rather than facilitating the legitimacy of one's actions, the strategic aim of *guanxi* is to enhance the reputation for the trustworthiness of actors by providing a series of situations in which they can continuously enact (as well as be evaluated on) their 'meeting the expectations of others' (Ho 1976: 873). Under the Confucian understanding of harmony, losing the trust of the other participating actors is the greatest danger to the relational world order enacted through the practices of *guanxi* (Huang and Shih 2014: 19). In this setting, it is not power (accumulation of material capabilities) that defines the patterns of international interactions, but rather the expectations (as well as obligations) engendered by a relationally constructed global life. Consequently, the insistence on the harmonious respect for the other can be read as nothing short of a strategic desire for the recognition of an actor's reputation profile on the world stage.[23]

Conclusion

This chapter has provided an overview of the concept of *guanxi* and the types of relationality afforded by its practices. Demonstrating its significance to Chinese intellectual traditions (not only about relationality), the analysis uncovers its implications for IR thought and action. The attention has been to uncovering some of the ways in which the concept of *guanxi* informs such relational IR theorizing. In particular, the contention of this chapter has been that the dynamic multiplicity of interdependent conditioning factors engenders an interpersonal realm whose complexity is only partially known to the participating actors. This outlook calls for a contextual attunement to the transient constellations of factors and actors that affect the content, trajectories, and possible transformations in any social relationship – regardless of whether they occur on an interpersonal, regional, or global level. In particular, the long-term orientation of *guanxi* inserts a modicum of predictability by lowering the transaction costs and ensuring the peaceful resolution of conflicts. The underlying aim is to aid the ability to engage an ever-changing world.

The decentring implicit in such an engagement draws attention to the idiosyncratic structural conditions and unique cultural categories that contribute to the participants' thinking about and involvement in interpersonal situations (Hwang 1987: 946). The claim then is that the encounter with the notion of *guanxi* evinces relational IR theorizing as an optics which both acknowledges the agency of 'others' and through which meanings are generated contingently through interactions in communities of practice, whose relations are premised on the variable reputations of participants and the necessity for ongoing reiteration of the commitment to do things together. In short, the contention of this chapter has been (a la Kwang-kuo Hwang) that IR's encounter with the concept and practices of *guanxi* helps it move beyond the assumption that the world is populated by isolated individual actors, who are socialized to make rational decisions on the basis of self-interest (Hwang 1987: 944). At the same time, the relationality backstopping such transactions emerges as a 'more effective strategy in the new "context of action", for diminishing asymmetries of power and countering those practice by means of competent, active, committed, and responsible participation in world affairs' (Russel and Tokatlian 2003: 17).

Thus, due to the dynamic nature of such interactions, what passes for world order is not only constantly changing, but demands ongoing commitment to participating in and maintaining relations. As will be elaborated in the conclusion of the book, the particular patterns of world affairs offer contextual figurations, contingent on the specificities of each interaction and yet, simultaneously, more than the sum of their parts. The very claim that the global life is relational and populated by and emerges through the continuous interactions between plentiful varieties of life and matter calls for the positing of alternative ontologies that exceed what is possible (and imaginable) under the substantialist and Eurocentric metanarrative of the IR mainstream. The concluding chapter of the book therefore evokes the registers of worlding mutuality by elaborating the ways in which *guanxi* can help transcend the Eurocentric instrumentalism of disciplinary inquiry. In other words, the 'international' so conceived emerges as a relational system brimming with social interactions rather than withdrawal from such exchanges.

Notes

1 Confirming this heterotopic position of China in Western intellectual thought, the German philosopher Hegel quipped that 'it would have been better had they [works of Chinese thought] never been translated' (Hegel 1995: 121). Likewise others point out that 'since Adam Smith's lurid depictions of Chinese paupers gratefully feasting on putrid animal carcasses in *The Wealth of Nations*, China

has served liberal economists as a negative *mirror-image* which reflects the superiority of the entrepreneurial spirit of the liberal "West" ' (Whyte 2017: 1). As Roland Boer (2015) observes, Adam Smith quite consciously deployed the image of China as not merely uncivilized, but 'more than "savage" ' in order to legitimize the 'structural racism' of his version of capitalism. Thus, Adam Smith's *The Wealth of Nations* went to depict China as 'Such nations, however, are so miserably poor, that, from mere want, they are frequently reduced . . . to the necessity sometimes of directly destroying, and sometimes of abandoning their infants, their old people, and those afflicted with lingering diseases, to perish with hunger, or to be devoured by wild beasts. Among civilised and thriving nations, on the contrary . . . the produce of the whole labour of the society is so great, that all are often abundantly supplied, and a workman, even of the lowest and poorest order, if he is frugal and industrious, may enjoy a greater share of the necessaries and conveniences of life than it is possible for any savage to acquire . . . The poverty of the lower ranks of people in China far surpasses that of the most beggarly nations in Europe. In the neighbourhood of Canton many hundred, it is commonly said, many thousand families have no habitation on the land, but live constantly in little fishing boats upon the rivers and canals. The subsistence which they find there is so scanty that they are eager to fish up the nastiest garbage thrown overboard from any European ship. Any carrion, the carcase of a dead dog or cat, for example, though half putrid and stinking, is as welcome to them as the most wholesome food to the people of other countries. Marriage is encouraged in China, not by the profitableness of children, but by the liberty of destroying them. In all great towns several are every night exposed in the street, or drowned like puppies in the water. The performance of this horrid office is even said to be the avowed business by which some people earn their subsistence' (quoted in Boer 2015).

2 The intention here is to make an analytical contribution to the understanding and explanation of the post-Western flavours of relationality in IR rather than illustrate how China has been able to gain a tremendous amount of goodwill and political capital in the Global South.

3 In the complex historical narratives of Chinese diplomatic cuisine, fishtails are symbols of improvement and good fortune, and the dish was supposed to indicate Mao's hope for a successful meeting (see 'At State Banquets, Food Is Potent Diplomatic Symbol', *Shanghai List*, 29 May 2014, p. B2). At the same time, Mao quite openly divulged to Nixon during their first meeting in February 1972 that 'I haven't been able to change it [China's ancient civilization]. I've only been able to change a few places in the vicinity of Beijing' (quoted in Kissinger 2011: 110).

4 Most commentators tend to take as their point of departure the etymology of the two characters that make *guanxi*: '*guan* means barriers and *xi* means connections' (Jia 2006: 49–54; Luo 1997: 49; Lee and Dawes 2005: 29). More specifically, *guan* designated a ' "wooden crossbar for doors", "strategic pass", "toll gate" ' or the activity of 'closing' or 'connecting', while *xi* used to refer to 'tie' or to 'care for' (Langenberg 2007: 5). The literal meaning of *guanxi* then was 'connection across barriers' or 'pass the gate and get connected' (Jia 2006: 49–54; Luo 1997: 49; Lee and Dawes 2005: 29). Metaphorically speaking, however, 'inside the door [or within the boundaries set by the barriers/toll gates] you may be "one of us", but outside the door your existence is barely recognized' (Luo 1997: 44). This inference should not be misunderstood as a suggestion

of a rigidly structured framework of exclusion (such as the one implied by the Danish term 'hygge', for instance). On the contrary, *guanxi* denotes openness to connections with other people and suggests a far more flexible and dynamic 'web of relationships that functions as the set of interlocking laces which connects people of different *weis* [positions/status]' (Hwang 1987: 963; Jia 2006: 49–54). It is also claimed that even though pragmatic, a *guanxi* relationship is profoundly infused with 'a higher sense of responsibility towards others' (Tong 2006: 309).

5 Although in circulation a century ago, the term was not deemed to be significant enough to warrant inclusion in the two classic Chinese dictionaries: the 1915 *ci yuan* ('sources of words') and the 1936 *ci hai* ('word sea') (Luo 1997: 44; Langenberg 2007: 4). This has urged some scholars to speculate whether there is anything distinctly 'Chinese' about *guanxi* or whether it is merely the Chinese stand-in for the general social phenomenon of reliance on favours to accomplish tasks (Gold et al. 2002: 13–14; Ledeneva 2008).

6 Some see a complex interplay between tradition and modernity in the distinction between the positive and negative aspects of *guanxi*. The positive connotation of *guanxi* is associated with its assistance for bottom-up and civil society empowerment by permitting 'individuals to use their social ingenuity to build a web of personal relationships' (Tsui and Farh 1997: 60). Called '*qinyou guanxi*', it is associated with more traditional dynamics aimed at the establishment of 'long-lasting webs of allegiance, serving to unite and strengthen the powerless' (Su and Littlefield 2001: 200; Tan and Snell 2002: 380). A number of commentators find the origins of this trend during the Maoist years in China, when *guanxi* networks provided ordinary people with opportunities to distance themselves from the oppressive state-saturated system, carve out room to manoeuvre and order their own lives (Yang 2002: 466). Thus, by engaging in alternative forms of solidarity, the relational power of *guanxi* allows those in asymmetrical relationships to subvert established hierarchies and to mitigate the dilemmas of over-regulation and the political pressures imposed on everyday life. The negative flavour of *guanxi* comes from its association with graft. In this respect, the very patterns that make *guanxi* a 'weapon of the weak' (Ledeneva 2008: 124; Yang 1994: 206) are also the key ingredients of its dark side. Yet rather than essentializing it as a cultural trait associated with Asian backwardness, this aspect of *guanxi* can be read as an idiosyncratic encounter between the forces of transnational capitalism and the economic development of the state (Yang 2002: 468). It tends to be associated with corrupt forms of rent seeking – more often than not by officials or persons in position of power (Su and Littlefield 2001: 200; Tan and Snell 2002: 380). This distinction also connects to the discussion of the relational self (see later). The distinction between 'a "greater self"' (*da wo*), on the one hand, representing filial piety and kinship networks, and a subordinate "lesser self"' (*xiao wo*) (Barbalet 2013: 662). According to Zhao Tingyang, the latter – more self-interested one – was always going to be secondary to the 'higher' ethical commitment of *guanxi*: 'never demanding too much; always leaving room for the unknown; and, most important, always taking others into consideration . . . briefly, never maximizing self-interest' (Zhao 2012: 50). In this setting, phrases such as 'crony capitalism' and 'Confucian nepotism' seem to overlook the socio-temporal contingency underpinning the bounds of obligation and networks of support that characterize the practices of *guanxi* (Yang 2002: 469–476). In fact, some have gone as far as to claim that

what (Western observers usually) criticize as the corrupt side of *guanxi* is in fact the misunderstood 'Confucian Ethic' of Asian capitalism (Luo 1997: 48). Max Weber would find the latter claim particularly difficult to stomach, as he was among the early Western critics of *guanxi* and argued that it would be one of the key factors hindering the development of market economic relations in China (Heffner 2008: 7).

7 As the earlier discussion demonstrates, both the positive and negative features of *guanxi* reflect an idiosyncratic coalescence between tradition and modernity – or what some have referred to as the 'critical inheritance and critical transformation of Chinese thought' (Liu 2014: 121) – in the process of achieving collective goals.

8 As the eminent Chinese scholar Liang Shiming has pointed out, the Chinese worldview is 'neither *geren benwei* (individual-based) nor *shehui benwei* (society-based), but *guanxi benwei* (relation-based)' (cited in Gold et al. 2002: 10).

9 Translating it to the level of the 'international', Feng Zhang eloquently argues that this framework imagines the structure of world order as always already conceived in relational terms. Thus, historically speaking, the 'Chinese state' had no moral purpose as such (i.e., it had 'no obligation of promoting Chinese civilization' because, in practice, it was 'neither a territorial state nor a homogeneous community'), but 'as a patrimonial household bound together by artificial kinship' – a rationalization, which entailed 'the profound moral purpose of bringing propriety, order, and peace to the world as one universal family presided over by the emperor as patriarch' (Zhang 2016: 159).

10 It seems to be a recent distortion to suggest that because of the pursuit of harmony [discussed in the following section], *guanxi* ties imply (and, in fact, demand) a complete subordination to authority. The Confucian underpinnings of *guanxi* expect authority to be challenged and held accountable; such stance demands 'remonstration, i.e. to demonstrate "loyal opposition", such as failure to "straighten them out" represents a breach of duty under Confucian precepts and thus failure to practice Confucian moral virtues' (Tan and Snell 2002: 370–375). Perhaps surprisingly, such stance appears more liberal and progressive than classical Western precepts of democracy, where proponents such as Immanuel Kant explicitly oppose resistance against authority – even when it is legitimate: 'all the incitements of the subjects to violent expressions of discontent, all defiance which breaks out in rebellion, is the greatest and most punishable crime in the commonwealth, for it destroys its very foundations. The prohibition is absolute. Even if the power of the state has violated the original contract, the subject is still not entitled to offer counter-resistance' (Kant 1991: 81).

11 In fact some stress that 'a singular feature of guanxi is that the exchanges tend to favour the weaker member. Guanxi links two persons, often of unequal ranks, in such a way that the weaker partner can call for special favours for which he does not have to equally reciprocate. An unequal exchange face (respect, honour) to the one who voluntarily gives more than he receives' (Alston 1989: 28; Luo 1997: 43). Others have suggested a certain paradox of power in *guanxi*, where due to the structure of reciprocal obligation 'the weaker party is effectively and paradoxically more powerful than the stronger' (Barbalet and Qi 2013: 412). Shih (2016: 9) makes a similar point by emphasizing the 'higher level of anxiety' that the presumed or aspiring great powers have in a relational context because of the constant need to receive affirmation for their reputational profile. At the same time, 'maintaining group harmony and integrity is much more important than is insisting on distributive equity' (Hwang 1987: 956).

12 A significant number of Chinese commentators have suggested that the emphasis on relationality is premised on a holistic worldview distinct from the Western dualistic opposition between self and other/self and the world (Qin 2007:
330). In Chinese scholarship such difference pivots on the contrast between
relational and autonomous self. Associated primarily with Western intellectual
traditions, the latter insists on discrete subjectivities, praises individualism, and
values and normalizes the lack of dependence on others. The relational self,
on the other hand, insists that individuals do not and cannot exist unless they
are enmeshed in relations with others. Thus, whereas the so-called Eurocentric
conceptualizations of identity have been associated with assumptions that the
individual has (or should have) absolute authority in making independent ethical judgements, the Confucian framing of *guanxi* suggests that 'the individual
is only considered an entity within a network of relationships' (Tan and Snell
2002: 361). It seems that the origins of this conceptualization can be traced back
to Confucius himself, for whom 'unless there are at least two human beings
there are no human beings' (Rosemont 2006: 11–17). The point about the relational self, however, is not to deny the existence of individuality, but that it is
a framing of individuality that is distinct from the dominant 'Western' ones.
As Roger T. Ames (1994: 197) reveals, this is 'a notion of unique individuality
rather than autonomous individuality'. Autonomy, in this context, denotes 'a
single, separate, and indivisible thing that by virtue of some essential property
or properties, qualifies as a member of a class', whereas uniqueness reflects 'the
character of a single and unsubstitutable particular'. The inference is that the
identification of such particularity can happen only relationally through and in
interactions. The relational self, thereby, is 'one which is intensely aware of the
social presence of other human beings' (Ho 1995:117). The interdependence
and reciprocity characterizing such relational self accords social relations much
greater significance, and relations are often seen as ends in and of themselves
rather than means for realizing various individual goals (Tsui and Farh 1997:
61; Farh et al. 1998: 473). The proposition is that the Chinese constitution of
self-identity is premised on and built around a network of roles and relationships
(Tan and Snell 2002: 362). That is to say that the self 'was never conceived of as
an isolated or isolatable entity' (Tu 1985: 53). With its sense of connectedness
and interdependence, the framing of the relational self involves an understanding that 'nobody has an essence, but can be defined only "co-relationally" at
any given time' (Ames and Rosemont 1998: 24). This take on the relational
self backstops 'the altogether social nature of human life, for the qualities of
persons, the kinds of persons they are, and the knowledge and attitudes they
have are not exhibited in actions, but only in *interactions*' (Rosemont 1991: 89;
emphasis in original). In this context, David Wong (2004: 420–421) offers two
explanations of the particularities of the Chinese framing of the relational self:
he labels the first one 'the social conception of the person' and the second one
he calls 'the developmental sense of relationality'. The former implies that 'we
begin life embodied as biological organisms and become persons by entering
into relationships with others of our kind'; and the latter suggests that 'persons
need the help of others to develop as agents' (Wong 2004: 420–421).

13 The claim of this study is that the relationality of *guanxi* is focused on the management of hostile role-playing in order to maintain the longevity of interactions. In particular, the proposition here is that role demands do not emerge
in the abstract, but are borne out of the process of interactions. Because roles

are circumstantial, the qualitative innovation emerging from the dynamics of *guanxi* is that an actor can play any role on the world stage, regardless of their identity. The emphasis on relationality is premised on a holistic worldview distinct from the Western dualistic opposition between self and other/self and the world (Qin 2007: 330). The 'focus is not fixed on any particular individual, but on the particular nature of the relations between individuals who interact with each other' (King 1985: 63). Such construction of the relational self reveals the 'Chinese worldview as an integrated system of subject and object: the individual is placed in the spatial-temporal location of the world, with her experiences, values, and expectations constantly shaping and being shaped by the world' (Liu 2011: 4). In this setting, it is the *guanxi* process itself (rather than the individuals involved) that has agency – namely, it is 'the "relation that selects"', meaning that relations shape an actor's identity and influence her behaviour' (Qin 2009: 9). Lucian Pye (1968: 174) sees in this dynamic the origins of the Chinese 'compulsive need to avoid disorder and confusion, to seek predictability and the comforts of dependency [which] makes them very anxious to seek any acceptable basis for orderly human relations'.

14 Not only the roles, per se, but the very ethical (and moral) inflections of interactions are relational and arise in the contingent context of exchanges rather than being pre-given: 'the rightness of acts depends on their being morally fitting in the circumstances and has little to do with the disposition or motive of the agent' (Lau 1979: 27).

15 This point draws on the analysis by Chen (2016). Chen, however, misses out on the dynamic processes of relationality that backstop these practices, which leads him to treat them as ossified and static structures of Chinese foreign policy making rather than as instances of fluid practices of interaction.

16 The point here is that *guanxi* ties, and the exchanges that define them, improve the flow of information among participants not merely because they offer a more flexible arrangement, but mainly because of their reliability. As will be explained in the following section, in a highly contextual (and context-dependent) society such as the one in China, trustworthiness (which, in its instrumental sense, is understood as a commitment to honour obligations to others) is ensured by the potential damage to one's social standing (or 'face'). Hence, the bonds of reputation (the ongoing assurance of one's social position through the continuous fulfilment of *guanxi* obligations) ensure the reliability of information, knowledge, and resources exchanged in the context of interaction – thus, introducing a modicum of predictability (Dunfee and Warren 2001). At the same time, *guanxi* ties can be used for multiple and diverse purposes, such as building resilience in the context of recognizing and influencing emergent opportunities (Kavalski 2012: 74; Pye 1995: 44).

17 As already indicated in Chapter 2, such framing of the 'logic of relationships' suggests that it is relations that are not only at the heart of the explanation and understanding of the world, but also central to its observation, interpretation, and encounter. On the one hand, relations (and the webs of interactions that they constitute) provide a platform for the exercise of power. On the other hand, relations themselves have power – namely, they frame future patterns of interaction (Qin 2009: 9). Informed by the extremely situational and particularistic nature of Chinese culture, the logic of relationships infers that as the circumstances of interactions change, so, too, will the patterns of *guanxi* (Pye 1995: 46). Such framing also undermines the linear causality backstopping Western takes on

relationality – namely, that if two (or more actors) interact with one another, their relations will necessarily lead to greater intimacy (Parks 1982). Rather than focusing on the personality or identity of participating actors, the logic of relationships suggests that the conditions for interaction "cannot be forced" and remain "largely *unknown* and *unknowable*" (Chang and Holt 1991: 54; emphasis in original). Thus, the process of interaction facilitates the likelihood of future relations (which is the key strategic function of *guanxi*) rather than intimacy. (Such a claim should not, however, be misunderstood as an assertion that the process is not affective. The point here is that *guanxi* is not about the subjective qualities of the participants, but about the process of interactions in which they are entangled and whose agency engenders the performance of their [contingent] roles). Ensuring the longevity of a particular relationship trumps the pursuit of immediate gains. As has already been stated in the preceding discussion, what is crucial about such logic of relationships is that as the hub of social knowledge and social life, the patterns of *guanxi* intimate that shared understandings are not imposed as rules, rights, or obligations, but emerge in and from the very process of interaction.

18 Wen and Wang (2013: 193–195) go on to elaborate the appropriateness of such interactions with the world through what they refer to as a broadening and deepening 'propensity of circumstance' – the ability to handle the spontaneous emergence of things as a result of sociality's contingency. Such propensity derives from the cultivation of a resonant capacity to respond to 'the context of the changing world'. It is thus, through continually 'improving our competence for coping with situations that gives us a sense of affecting order and harmony' (Wen and Wang 2013: 193–195). At the same time, others have pointed out that the cultivation of such resonant capacities reflects processes of self-understanding 'through relations and contexts' (Lai 2008: 4–7). The 'games of harmony' are not (and can never be) zero-sum games (Zhao 2012: 51).

19 *Guanxi* thereby presages an understanding of international action and agency – both cognitively and affectively – as simultaneously shaped and mediated by ethical obligations and commitments to others (the structure and content of which are acquired through the very relationships by which ethical obligations and commitments to others are disclosed). Such a framing yet again reiterates the Confucian (among others) frameworks of the relational self, which suggest that the relational self can occupy multiple social roles simultaneously and gains fulfilment through living within multiple webs of relations.

20 Due to the contextual ubiquity of *guanxi*, foreign policy making becomes a contingent outcome of relational interactions between actors – that is, the relational context frames the policy response, but because of its inherent fluidity, policy is expected to fluctuate (Zhang 2015: 211).

21 Leadership Studies offers worthwhile narrative metaphors that help frame communities of practice as co-authored relational texts, engendering 'a shift in our understanding of organizations as "things" towards experiencing them more as an array of stories, always in the act of construction whose meaning and relevance is context-dependent. Meaning is constantly negotiated and renegotiated in the relational act of conversation, deriving its meaning within the context of its sociocultural location. The world is seen as being brought into being via our collaborative "storying" of our experience' (Abell and Simmons 2000: 161).

22 It is in this setting that *xinyong* (trustworthiness) – the reputation for meeting one's obligations to others – gains its significance as 'the most valuable asset'

in the transactional web of *guanxi* (DeGlopper 1995: 205–206). Thus, rather than facilitating the legitimacy of one's actions, the strategic aim of *guanxi* is to enhance the trustworthiness of actors by providing a series of situations in which they can continuously enact (as well as be evaluated on) their 'meeting the expectations of others' (Ho 1976: 873). Under the conditions of harmony, losing the trust of the other participating actors is the greatest danger to the gimballed world order envisioned by the relationality of *guanxi* (Huang and Shih 2014: 19). In this setting, Chinese insistence on the harmonious respect for the other can be read as nothing short of a strategic desire for status recognition. Motivated by the insecure status associated with the relational constitution of international interactions, the operational beliefs of *guanxi* provide ongoing modalities for engendering trust by demonstrating China's capacity and willingness to meet its obligations to others.

23 This is an aspect that will be elaborated on at length in the conclusion of this book.

Conclusion
A relational theory of international relations beyond the Eurocentric frame

Introduction

The intent of this book has been to construct a relational theory of IR with the help of the concept and practices of *guanxi*. The point of departure for this journey of healing IR from its Columbus syndrome is the itinerant translation of the Congress of Vienna. The claim is that the standard narrative of the Congress in IR furnishes the foundation stone for the substantialist and Eurocentric worldview of the discipline. During nine months, from November 1814 to June 1815, the participants at the Congress 'waltzed' and 'feasted' their way to an agreement on the post-Napoleonic international order. However, rather than a complex and nuanced 'dance', IR narrates the experience of the Congress through the metaphor of a formal and impersonal 'concert' of Europe. Chapter 1 therefore recalled the relationality – and, in particular, the social practices, reciprocal figurations, and personal interconnections – which have been (seemingly carefully) excluded from the standard narrative. To the extent that it functioned, the Concert system was a contingent social practice made possible by fluid iterations of social transactions that percolated and gained salience in the context of ongoing and multiple relations during the nine months of the Congress. Just like the Viennese waltz, whose movements are always already different, global life not only moves in mysterious ways, but in the process it transforms, changes, and adapts in ways that cannot be anticipated in advance (and whose very patterns and practices adjust and change continuously and unexpectedly).

Chapter 2 then reviewed two of the most prominent conversations on relationality in IR – those in its Anglophone and Sinophone variants. According to the proponents of these two branches of the 'larger family of *relational social theory*' (Jackson and Nexon 2017: 1; emphasis in original), the mechanistic (and nearly clockwork) features of the substantialist imaginary that dominates the IR mainstream discloses a normalization of oppression evidenced by the control, domination, and exploitation of various others – be they human (indigenous, non-Western, and other vulnerable communities) or non-human (nature, species, and objects). To be sure, some international phenomena – especially when treated in isolation – may appear orderly at times (that is, predictable, rational, and linear); however, the point of the proponents of the relational turn is that systemically global politics as a whole is defined by non-linearity, recursivity, and unpredictability. Thus, by painting itself in the substantialist corner, the disciplinary mainstream has, on the one hand, evaded the need to recognize that there are dynamics which are not only unknown, but probably cannot ever be meaningfully rendered comprehensible, and, on the other hand, has stifled endeavours that can engage in thoughtful deliberation of the discontinuities, unpredictability, and non-linearity of global life (Kavalski et al. 2018).

In this setting, Chapter 3 offered a dialogue between the Anglophone and Sinophone conversations on relationality. Drawing on the concept and practices of *guanxi*, the analysis amplifies the intrinsic relationality of global life and the realms of IR. In contrast to the dualistic bifurcations that dominate IR imaginaries, the encounter and engagement with concepts such as *guanxi* both illuminate and remind the study of world affairs that the complex patterns of global life resonate with the fragility, fluidity, and mutuality of global interactions, rather than the static and spatial arrangements implicit in the fetishized currency of self–other/centre–periphery/ hegemon–challenger models underpinning the binary metanarratives of IR. This is a major departure from the current state of the art on relationality in IR; rather than looking at dyadic sets of relations as well as the identities and capacity of individual actors, the preceding engagement with *guanxi* inheres an IR pivoted on webs of figurations intertwined by a conscious and strategic search for relations with others. International actors are not just isolated entities moving about in the vacuum of world affairs; instead, they are entangled in and produced by multitudes of relations among and across many different spatio-temporal contexts. In this respect, actors (and their agency) have effects only to the extent that they are *in relations* with others. At the same time, the notion of relationality suggests that the interactions of global life are not just self-organizing and co-constitutive, but that they can hardly be regulated.

Thus, due to the dynamic nature of such interactions, what passes for world order is not only constantly changing, but demands ongoing commitment to participating in and maintaining relations. It is thereby a contextual figuration, contingent on the specificities of each interaction and yet, simultaneously, more than the sum of their parts. The very claim that the global life is relational and populated by and emerges through the continuous interactions between plentiful varieties of life and matter calls for the positing of alternative ontologies that exceed what is possible (and imaginable) under the substantialist and Eurocentric metanarrative of the IR mainstream. With this in mind, the concluding section of the book offers a relational reading of China's rise before sketching some of the implications for a relational IR theorizing beyond the Eurocentric frame.

The relationality of China's rise

How to think about and theorize China? Current preoccupations with the 'rise of China' attest to the nascent contestation of the very idea of what the pattern of international politics should look like and how it should be practiced. More than a century ago, the American scholar and diplomat Paul S. Reinsch observed that the 'suddenness with which the entire perspective of the political world has been changed by China is unprecedented. That country, without question, has become the focal point of international politics' (Reinsch 1900: 83). Such statements illustrate the complex dynamic of continuity and change in world affairs – thus, although the individual elements that form the context of Reinsch's proclamation have changed significantly from his day, the broader patterns of interaction that it refers to appear to show remarkable resilience. In particular, China's expanding outreach and diversifying roles have provided a novel context for the ongoing reconsiderations of world affairs and their governance. In the wake of the Cold War, commentators were pondering how far Western ideas would spread in a geopolitical environment characterized by 'the end of history'. Today, the debate seems to be not only the expanse of Chinese investments, but also how far Chinese ideas will reach (Horesh and Kavalski 2014; Deng 2008; Harnish et al. 2016; Shih 2013; Yu 2012).

Few, however, have pondered whether and how China's rise may pose *theoretical* challenges to the way we make sense of China and world politics more broadly. If anything, when it comes to understanding China's rise, the most commonly applied theoretical frameworks seem to be some of the most orthodox IR theories, with power transition theory and offensive realism readily coming to mind.[1] It has to be stated at the outset that this endeavour should not be misunderstood as an attempt to overthrow existing paradigms and perspectives. Instead, it draws attention to the realization that there are distinct and newly emerging modes and models of global politics as well as ways for their explanation, understanding, and interpretation that require a pluriverse of epistemological and ontological lenses (Agathangelou and Ling 2009; Chan et al. 2001; Crawford and Bleiker 2001; Crawford and Javies 2001; Ling 2015). If democracy has indeed become 'the fundamental standard of political legitimacy in the current era' (Held 2004), it is to be expected that the (con)current 'democratization' of international relations would enunciate a cacophony of voices promoting alternative visions of the 'appropriate' forms of legitimation and authority in global life. In particular, the heuristics of *guanxi* suggest that shifts in material capabilities do not in and of themselves reveal much about the patterns of world affairs unless they are assessed in their interactive environment. Drawing on the narratives of power transition, the story of China's rise takes as its point of departure the dyad of hegemon–challenger – the former unwilling to relinquish its leadership position, whereas the latter has growing capacities and aspirations to claim it (by force, if necessary). The impoverished Cartesian outlook of this IR narrative prescribes the transformation of generic fears into specific threats which then inform policies of alliance building or offer opportunities for military conquest.[2] It is therefore not surprising that more often than not the discussion of China's rise turns into a conversation about if and when a Sino-American military conflict would likely erupt.

The alternative narrativization provided by a relational IR theorizing treats China's rise as a socially negotiated practice (for which power transition offers, at best, only a partial label). It would be a mistake to assume that such relational reading proscribes antagonism or confrontation. (Radical) difference – such as the one associated with the phenomenon of China's rise and the episteme of *guanxi* – is the very condition for the possibility of emergence and innovation in global life. Thus, rather than something that needs to be controlled, subjugated, or denied, the difference of China's rise can be translated through the relational lens of 'interdependence-in-antagonism' – a normative stance that treats cooperation and competition as corresponding forces which underpin the mutual dependence of all those inhabiting global life (Patomäki 2002: 62; Kavalski 2018b: 207–221). Thus, rather than a condition requiring ongoing securitization, difference discloses 'a relation that brings disagreements into the conversation and forces the mechanisms that proscribe other forms of being and knowing to become visible' (Rojas 2016: 380). For instance, as illustrated in Chapter 1, the contextual and complicated interactions of the dancing relationality that emerged at the Congress of Vienna disturbs the 'billiard-ball' notion of causality implicit in the standard IR narrative of the Concert of Europe:

> Perception, valuation, motivation, and strategic calculation, for example, are cognitive developments that emerge through chains of relations, as are structures of relation and structures of meaning. Thus, while ideas, values, rational choices and calculations, motives, and dispositions may be consequential in guiding behaviour or action, they are not autonomous forces. They are, rather, elements that operate within and gain salience in the context of social relations [or what I refer in

this book as 'the context of doing things together']. Relations are the contents that connect interacting parties and actors and can shape the form and functions of their interactions (i.e., potentially constructive, but also potentially destructive, as is usually the case in interactions devoid of contacts, ties, and exchange of information). They provide the context for strategic calculations, subjective interpretations, and more often than not, dispositions, and they mediate the degree to which these elements shape behaviour.

(Alimi et al. 2015: 26)

In this respect, from a relational point of view, both the international identity and status of international actors are connected to and constitutively imbricated in the enactments and articulations of specific roles in the context of communities of practice.[3] China thus seems to posit a pattern of relations, normativity steeped in the 'singularly historical practice of universal principles that is open to emulation not as a universal pattern, but for its procedures in articulating the universal to concrete historical circumstances' (Dirlik 2012: 291). The point here is that rather than relying on the atomistic models provided by power transition theory, the relationality uncovered in this book suggests that what we are witnessing is a struggle for recognition among multiple actors trying to assert their normative power position. According to Ian Manners' oft-quoted definition, normative powers are only those actors who can 'shape what can be "normal" in international life'. As he insists (and few would disagree) 'the ability to define what passes for "normal" in world politics is, ultimately, the greatest power of all' (Manners 2002: 253). The proposition here is that the definitions of the 'normal' are not merely undertaken by normative power, but they emerge in the context of its interaction with others. Recognition, in this setting, is indicated by the specific reactions of target states. In this respect, the issue is not merely about *being* and *becoming* a normative power, but also about being recognized as one by others.

Even though they are 'self-made international actors', the suggestion is that normative power is not entirely an intrinsic property of an actor, but depends on the kind of interactions it engenders in specific contexts and the way such interactions frame the responses of its interlocutors (Kavalski 2013: 249). Thus, the phenomenon of China's rise can be read through a *desire to be recognized* as an actor that is not only capable, but who also has the right to set the ramifications of the "normal" in global life. Yet for such normative power claim to have legitimacy, Beijing has to be considered to behave in certain ways to earn such recognition – to borrow from the language of *guanxi*, Beijing needs to have a reputation for fulfilling its obligations towards others. Thus, the viability of the so-called 'China model' is not entirely dependent on decisions taken in Beijing, but contingent on the interpretation of its agency by its interlocutors. In this respect, actors (and their agency) have effects only to the extent that they are *in relations* with others. Due to the dynamic nature of such interactions, what passes for world order is not only constantly changing, but demands ongoing commitment to participating in and maintaining relations.

Normative powers are only 'partial agents' – that is, in an international environment defined by constant flux, the ability to define the 'normal' is subject to ongoing negotiation in which 'the parties learn about each other and themselves' (Paltiel 2009: 206; Kavalski and Cho 2015: 443). In this setting, *recognition* emerges as 'the core constitutive moment' of international interactions and refers to 'the communicative process in the international society of states through which states mutually acknowledge the status and social esteem of other states' (Nel 2010: 963). The acknowledgement of such a nascent struggle for recognition suggests that the contestation between normative powers moves beyond their relative capability – that is, it cannot be captured through the narratives of 'struggle for power'. In other words, the answer to the question 'Who or what exists politically as a normative power?' is 'Those actors that are *recognized* as normative powers'. Recognition, in this setting, is indicated by the specific attitudes, dispositions, and behaviour of target states. Due to the inherent insecurity of the struggle for recognition, international actors attempt to take control over the process of meaning creation by anchoring their identity to explicit material practices (Kavalski 2013: 258). What distinguishes normative powers is their willingness to create and improvise in the context of ongoing and contingent interactions rather than rely on the provision of prescriptive or proscriptive solutions. It has to be acknowledged that such relational framing of normative powers will make the explanation and understanding of IR doubtlessly messy, but it also promises to heal the habits of control, manipulation, and exploitation associated with IR's insistence on the separation between subject and object, knower and known, self and other, mind and matter.

Thus, in the complexity of global life, the recognition *by* others rests on recognition *of* others (Kavalski 2007). In this context, the reference to normative power indicates an actor's ability to show consideration for the effects of its actions on others. As suggested, China's respect for the other encourages expectations of reciprocity. It goes beyond the mere acknowledgement of an actor's 'equal membership rights' and involves 'an appreciation about what is distinct and valuable' about this actor (Nel 2010: 965). Consequently, global life is both conceived of as 'a complex plurality of ideas, views, and values' and distinguished by 'a plurality of political identities in search of recognition' (Hurrell 2007: 10). The point here is that while indeed global life is marked by multiple pluralities, when it comes to recognition, at issue is not so much the identity of international actors, but their roles (and, in particular, how well they are perceived to discharge them). At the same time, it has to be reminded that such recognition is both tentative and revocable and attests to the 'constitutive vulnerability' of international actors – especially normative powers – to 'the unpredictable reactions and responses of others' (Kavalski 2013: 259). This suggestion does not deny that the relationship is asymmetrical; yet the status of China as a normative power is premised on having others' acknowledgement – that is, it is a two-way process. The point is that material asymmetries do not translate neatly into a relational one. International interactions are volitional, and the structure of hierarchy should not be misunderstood as giving one side influence over the other. On the contrary, the very nature of reciprocal obligation belies its constraining power on all participants in a relationship. Thus, the ability to treat others with respect allows normative powers to gain the recognition that creates the permissive environment allowing them to define and redefine the standards of the 'normal' in international life. Thus, the international identity of an actor is not just about capabilities, but mostly about recognition – which is both an outcome and a reassertion of an actor's normative power.

The relationality of post-Western IR

The implication from this emphasis on relationality is that by removing the veil of Eurocentrism, the endeavours of the post-Western project in IR reveal the impossibility to consider issues of ethics, ontology, epistemology, and politics in separation and as if they are not mutually implicated in one another. In other words, relationality extends a normative gesture aimed at 'imagining politics organized otherwise' (Kavalski et al. 2018). In terms of the epistemic difference of *guanxi*, the claim here is that such nonbinary relationality has become a defining feature of post-Western IR theory building and knowledge production (Bilgin and Ling 2017; Chen 2011; Eun 2016; Ling 2015). It seems few today would dispute that the disciplinary inquiry of IR is indelibly marked by the 'colonial signs' of its Eurocentric makeup. Not only that, but the 'apple pie' flavour that IR acquired in the context of its Cold War transformation into an 'American social science' seems to have made the discipline even more inimical towards encounters with the various non-Western others that its outlook consciously occludes. As a result, much of the IR mainstream rests on a 'disembodied understanding of knowledge', which relies on ongoing practices of abstraction and decontextualization that are central to the Eurocentric bifurcation backstopping the metanarrative of IR (Kavalski et al. 2018).

The mode of relationality advanced by this book offers a rare analytical bridge between the so-called Anglophone (Western/Global North/Eurocentric) and Sinophonic (but also, and broadly conceived, non-Western/Global South) traditions. At the same time, it uncovers their co-constitutive hybridity, mutuality, and reciprocal imbrication. Such a move strives to overcome the tendencies of both Eurocentrism and Sinocentrism by encouraging productive conversations and contestations between different modalities of being, thought, and action while illuminating 'the mutual cultural penetrations in which both Chinese and Western ways of thinking would have to change in light of new experiences and imaginaries in the age of globalization and cultural pluralism' (Liu 2014: 121). In an attempt to trouble the juxtapositions of temporal and geographical difference that still seem to stump any IR alternative prefixed by a 'non-' or a 'post-', this study posits the centrality of relationality as a distinguishing feature of all such projects. According to such mode of inquiry, the encounter with this more complex and contingent global life reveals a humbler epistemology, which simultaneously provokes and directs inquiries toward 'what are still possible empirical descriptions, but without the hubris of predicting linear outputs from linear inputs' (Kavalski et al. 2018). After all, a relational approach always takes the interactions and the circumstances in which they occur as its point of departure; consequently, the assumption is that goals, ends, and means are not pre-given (or a priori), but 'develop coterminously within contexts that are themselves ever changing and thus always subject to re-evaluation' (Emirbayer and Mische 1998: 967–968).

Thus, by painting itself in the Eurocentric corner, the disciplinary mainstream has, on the one hand, evaded the need to recognize that there are dynamics which are not only unknown, but probably cannot ever be meaningfully rendered comprehensible, and, on the other hand, has stifled endeavors that can engage in thoughtful deliberation of the discontinuities, unpredictability, and non-linearity of global life. In this setting, the relationality lens helps outline the contested terrain of post-Western IR as a space for dialogical learning, which encourages engagement with the possibilities afforded by the interactions of multiple worlds and privileges the experiences and narratives of neither of them (Kavalski 2012: 19). Such mode of theorizing allows building solidarity between like-minded projects targeting the silencing, hegemony, patriarchy, and violence of the mainstream by treating them as second-order aspects deriving from a first-order problematique – IR's poignant ontological and epistemic *lack of relationality*.[4] It is the very denial of relationality (first-order issue) that perpetuates the imperial, patriarchal, and racist attitudes (second-order issues) of IR. It is in this vein that the attack on the latter that so much of critical, feminist, and postcolonial theorizing undertakes overlooks the very condition of its possibility – the lack of relationality in IR. What this means is that the IR mainstream has been dominated by an atomistic understanding of global life which prioritizes fixed units of analysis (nation-states) and their discrete dyadic interactions (conflict/balancing in the context of anarchy). Yet at no point is the option of a sociability infused with the contingent opportunities inherent in the encounter with the other acknowledged in this narrative – let alone the potential that the phenomena and processes animating world affairs are mutually co-constituted in relation to one another. Instead, global life is envisioned as a domain of disconnected states, infamously imagined as billiard balls – 'closed, impermeable, and sovereign unit[s], completely separated from all other states' (Wolfers 1962: 19).

The substantialism backstopping the Eurocentric imagination of this image is framed by the perception that international life is a closed system of discrete sovereign actors whose interactions are subject to plausible calculations and predictable behaviours. The issue with this framing of the 'international' is not so much sovereignty, but the particular 'form it takes vis-à-vis the multiplicity that is identified as the threat. Sovereignty would here be the ability to arbitrate a topology within which it can exclusively intervene, thereby selectively perturbing a network, a circulation that is already self-governing' (Thacker 2009: 149). Thus, the recognition of the reliance on epistemic frameworks that privilege the substantialism of Eurocentric concerns assists in uncovering the pervasive inability of IR to account for the diverse modes of being, presence, and participation that are manifested in and comprise the social enmeshments of global life. In this setting, going beyond the Eurocentric frame incites IR to abandon its striving for full security, complete control, and insistence on the predictability of global life and its multiplicity. This should not be misunderstood as a call for the abandonment of the Anglosphere of IR – to do that would be tantamount to calling for and instituting a new type of substantialism. The relational mode of inquiry proposed in this book merely calls for acknowledging that the Eurocentric impositions of 'egotistic, autonomous actors are a fiction of Enlightenment philosophy' (Lebow 2003: 360).

This kind of a relational endeavour promises the development of an IR able to sustain complexity, foster dynamism, encourage the cross-pollination of disparate ideas, and engage the plastic and heterogeneous processes that periodically overwhelm, intensify, and infect (while all the time animating) the interactions of global life (Anker 2014: 454). Global life – just like life in general – is profoundly relational and has a tendency to pass, flow, and connect (meaning that it can move, relate, transform, and become) beyond boundaries and across limits (Ansems de Vries 2015: 75). Thus, in contrast to the dominant preoccupations of

> Western critical theory on 'individual human freedom and its relationship to political community', Chinese relationalism emphasizes

relationality understood as relationships of affection and obligation and their contribution to the formation of a humane international community. Both have a humanitarian spirit. But whereas modern Western humanitarianism stresses individual freedom, relational humanitarianism highlights mutual affection and support in an interconnected web of community relationships.

(Zhang 2016: 180)

In other words, relationality suggests modes for understanding, explanation, and encounter that are simultaneously attuned and open to the contradictions, challenges, and opportunities of a dynamic and unpredictable global life.

Conclusion: the molecular gimbal of global life and IR theory

With the help of the relational lens outlined in the preceding chapters, this book contends that thinking beyond the Eurocentric frames of IR urges 'us to connect the questions of political possibility with the dynamics and the intransigence of vast domains that are themselves recalcitrant to the purchase of politics' and, at the same time, acts as a provocation 'to imagine worlds both before and after us' (Clark 2014: 27–28). Such a move draws on a tradition of intellectual wondering and trespassing which does not subscribe to linear logics of detachment, coherence, and parsimony (Kavalski 2007). Yet, due to its Columbus syndrome, instead of engaging in such travelling, the substantialism which informs mainstream IR theory still refuses to recognize 'other' forms of theory building that go beyond its Eurocentric frame. In fact, such alternatives are sources for deep-seated anxiety:

Crossroads seem to have been one of the earliest and perhaps one of the most permanent fears of mankind. For it is alarming for anyone who knows his own weakness to contemplate whom we might be meeting at the next crossroad – friend or foe, weaker or stronger than he.

(Gottmann 1952: 517)

In order to rectify this trend, the kinds of relational thought and action envisioned with the help of the concept of *guanxi* insist that rather than being fearful of analytical crossroads and the unexpected encounters that they presage, IR should embrace the uncertainty attendant in the journey beyond the Eurocentric partitioning of the world. As the preceding chapters illustrate, such a move has palpable relational flavours associated with the convivial, yet dissonant, cross-pollination of values, narratives, and practices

in the study of global life. Such endeavours are backstopped by the generation of new modes of thought opposing 'the symmetry of an economy of
truth and understanding' with 'the radical asymmetry of an opening into the
unknown and unknowable' (Clark 2011: 74; Blanchot 1995: 5).

In particular, the relational study of world politics seeks to challenge what
can be termed as the *Eurocentric instrumentalism* of the discipline. In many
ways, the very claim that the world is populated by and emerges through the
continuous interactions between plentiful varieties of life and matter calls
for the positing of alternative ontologies of IR. Thus, by demonstrating the
'radical interdependence', mutual co-constitution, and embeddedness of a
multiplicity of figurations of relations, the interlocutors of the relational dialogues in IR seek to disrupt the linear reductionism of IR's ontological purview (Kavalski 2018b). The 'problem-solving' impulse backstopping the
Eurocentric predilections of IR reveals a certain degree of wishful thinking
in the disciplinary mainstream that global issues are not only 'amenable to
the identification of a clear linear causation', but also that what matters in
the study of world politics are phenomena that can be observed through such
a 'deterministic mode of efficient linear inquiry' (Kavalski et al. 2018). In
this respect, the ' "realties" that inform both the materiality of the world and
by extension the realms of IR are characterized as self-organizing, intrinsi-
cally relational, permeable, shifting, open-ended, and always historically
and geographically situated (thus contingent) properties' (Kavalski 2018a).
In the words of an intellectual fellow traveller: 'Realpolitik, geared toward
extreme maximization of self-interest, disrupts long-term relational stability. *Relational-politik*, as an ethically more defensible alternative may lead
international relations toward a more cooperative and harmonious direction'
(Zhang 2015: 182; emphasis in original).

The proposition here is that the relationality outlined in the preceding
chapters engenders a rather gimballed view of global life. Just like a ship's
compass – or a gimbal – the patterns of world affairs are made up of multiple, interdependent, and constantly shifting spheres of relations. Consequently, which resources get to be mobilized is a function not just of the
agency of specific actors, but also of the contingent interactions in which
they find themselves entangled. The gimballed framework differs from
the centre–periphery/hegemon–challenger/North–South/etc., models not
purely as a function of its relationality, but because of its relationality, it
asserts global life as a fluid dynamic rather than an innately spatial metaphor (pivoted on entities in constant opposition to one another). The result
is a multi-scalar framing of global life in which diverse layers of actors
and agency (and the various systems, institutions, and matter which they
inhabit) animate overlapping levels of contingent aggregation. Redolent
of the practices of *guanxi*, such a gimballed outlook advances a resilient

global life through openness to change.[5] At the same time, such a gimballed outlook suggests a radical reconsideration of the Eurocentric certainties dominating the purview of the discipline. The focus here is not only on acknowledging, but working creatively *with* and *through* the 'circles of reciprocal implication' (Coles 2016: 49) and the 'mutual encroachment of thousands and thousands of tendencies' (Bergson 2005: 281) engendered by such relationality.[6] Therefore, the attention is on the ways in which the affordances of relationality are foreshadowed or foreshortened by the post-Western turn in IR. Motivated by a commitment to 'dialogical imagination', such a gimballed outlook prompts comparisons, reflections, critiques, and understanding that 'combine contradictory certainties', while thriving on the contingency of interactions (Swaine 2013: 48). The encounter with the gimbal of global life thereby acts as a reminder that knowledge (not just IR knowledge) is acquired and mediated relationally through diverse sets of practices. By acknowledging its 'belonging to the world', such an approach calls for productive encounters with the multiple narratives of global life and the ever-changing and polyphonous global life (Agathangelou and Ling 2009).

In such a relational setting, IR becomes a project of disclosure – on the one hand, disclosing worlds and possibilities foreclosed by its Eurocentric bias and, on the other hand, disclosing the inextricable and invariable intertwinement between understanding, explanation, practices, and encounters in the study of world affairs. Understood as 'forces that are at once disruptive of the organization of the state and other dominant structures and creative of different modes of living and political potentialities', the patterns of relationality disclosed through the encounter with the concept and practices of *guanxi* develop creative alternative perspectives on both global life and the connections, mixtures, ruptures, and transactions animating the heterogeneous elements and forces percolating through its entangled figurations (Ansems de Vries 2015: 83). A *relational IR theorizing* – which is non-binary in the sense that it does not treat the West and the non-West as discrete and disconnected homogenous opposites, but as intertwined and mutually constitutive webs of interactions – proposes a molecular outlook whose unit of analysis is relations (rather than actors) and their multiple triadic dynamics (which open numerous and numinous points of and possibilities for interaction). It is relations that are not only at the heart of explaining and understanding the gimbal of global life, but also central to its observation and encounter. At the same time, relations are neither asserted nor imagined as pre-defined totalities. The epistemic verso of a *relational IR* is about the cultivation of attentiveness to the self-organizing, shifting, and historically and geographically contingent realities of a mobile and relational global life.

Such attentiveness will make IR research doubtlessly messy. Theorizing in this setting is not about the provision of knowledge in the sense of a positivistic measuring exercise that we have since the Enlightenment – rather, it is about forming than purely informing; it is about the art of living than de-contextual and detached abstract thought. In other words, relational knowledge production is incoherent and socially mediated – just like global life. Relational theorizing as the concept and practices of *guanxi* suggest is about knowledge that is embedded in repertoires of interaction. Messiness is needed if IR is to recover a disposition for encounter and engagement with the currents, trends, and voices that are occluded, uncomfortable, and not easily digestible by established paradigms. Thus, the encounter with the concept and practices of *guanxi* invokes the complexity of possible worlds uncovered by relational IR theorizing. In particular, it suggests that IR scholars and IR scholarship would do well to abandon their reliance on universalistic categories of international interactions and delve into the context and experiences of such relations and how they are played out in the everyday practices of global life. Going back to the experience of the so-called China's rise to global prominence (as a phenomenon, narrative, and a set of processes), it reminds us that global life is not necessarily a place where international actors merely find themselves in; it is where they get lost in the complexity of interactions and relationships.[7]

Notes

1   It is perhaps puzzling that these frameworks tend to overlook the relational qualities of power. As Harold Lasswell eloquently put it, at the end of the day, the study of politics boils down to 'who gets what, when, and how' (Lasswell 1936) – that is, it is about the opportunity, ability, and willingness to produce intended effects. However, although Lasswell's framing of power is one of the most quoted in the literature, his emphasis on the relational character of power often remains overlooked – namely, the 'intended effects' emerge in the context of distinct 'interpersonal situations' (Lasswell 1948: 10). Such emphasis on the interpersonal situation of power led him to conclude that world politics 'can assume no static certainty; it can only strive for dynamic techniques of navigating the tides of insecurity generated within the nature of man in culture' (Lasswell 1935: 217). Thus, to paraphrase the popular adage, if two international actors are to tango on the world stage, their dance is choreographed by the status of insecurity implicit in the demand for an ongoing recognition of the complex power relations that frame the score of the turbulent rhythm of their footsteps (Kavalski 2008).

2   In fact, the literature on *guanxi* offers a relational modality for reframing the narrative of the power transition theory (PTT) as a contest over the process of meaning generation. As Scott C. Hammond and Lowell M. Glenn note: 'Chaos could then be defined as a disruption of meanings brought about by new information . . . When meaning changes, conflict over new meanings may occur. Those privileged by the old meanings want to hold on, while those wanting to explore

the new meanings engage in a dialogic inquiry' (Hammond and Glenn 2004: 29). This framing echoes Pierre Bourdieu's insistence on the performative significance of language: 'the categories of perception, the schemata of classification, that is, essentially, the words, the names which construct social reality as much as they express it, are the same par excellence of political struggle, which is struggle to impose the legitimate principle of vision and division' (Bourdieu 2002: 123).

3 In particular, if we are to go back to the waltzing motions undergirding the practices of the Concert of Europe, the role of governing a particular set of international interactions (and their figurations) belies the patterns of 'relational authority, which treats authority as a social contract in which a governor provides a political value to a community in exchange for compliance by the governed with rules necessary to produce the order' (Loke 2010: 587).

4 The following distinction between first-order and second-order issues and atomistic vs. molecular outlooks borrows from Barbalet (2015) and Kavalski (2015).

5 This aspect borrows from Margaret Byrne Swaine's discussion of 'Chinese cosmopolitanism' and especially her elaboration of '*shijie zhuyi* (世界主义) – outward-looking engagement with the changing world, literally "worldism"' (Swaine 2013: 33–37).

6 Relationality in this gimballed sense is close to what Leonie Ansems de Vries calls 'milieu': 'a complex play of forces, including movements that constitute a medium of action for its governance; and movements in-between that both underlies and disrupts such order(ing)s . . . a play of forces of ordering and disordering, becoming and stratification, politics and depoliticization, in which space and time are operative dimensions, and in which new things-forces emerge, and become embedded in *and-or* fundamentally disruptive of the changing play of milieus' (Ansems de Vries 2015: xxii–xxiv; emphasis in original).

7 The last part of this statement echoes Aimé Césaire's poignant words that 'There are two ways to lose oneself: walled segregation in the particular or dilution in the "universal". My conception of the universal is a universal enriched by all that is particular, a universal enriched by every particular; the deepening and coexistence of all particulars' (Césaire [1956] 2010: 151).

Bibliography

Abbenhuis, Maartje (2014). *The Age of Neutrals*. Cambridge: Cambridge University Press.

Abbott, Andrew D. (1996a). Things of Boundaries. *Social Research* 62(3), 857–882.

Abbott, Andrew D. (1996b). *Time Matters*. Chicago, IL: Chicago University Press.

Abell, Ellen and Simmons, Shoshana (2000). How Much You Can Bend Before You Break. *European Journal of Work and Organizational Psychology* 9(2), 159–175.

Abott, Kenneth A. (1970). *Harmony and Individualism*. Taipei: Orient Cultural Service.

Acharya, Amitav (2000). Ethnocentrism and Emanipatory IR Theory. In Samantha Arnold and J. Marshall Beier, eds., *(Dis)Placing Security :Critical Re-Evaluations of the Boundaries of Security Studies/Samantha Arnold and J. Marshall Beier*. Toronto, ON: Centre for International and Security Studies, 1–18.

Adanir, Fikret (2016). The Congress of Vienna. In Katrin Boeckh and Sabina Rutar, eds., *The Balkan Wars*. Basingstoke: Palgrave Macmillan, 12–56.

Agathangelou, Anna and Ling, L.H.M (2009). *Transforming World Politics*. London: Routledge.

Albert, Mathias (2016). *A Theory of World Politics*. Cambridge: Cambridge University Press.

Alimi, Eltan Y., Demetriou, Chares and Bosi, Lorenzo (2015). Theorizing and Comparing Radicalization. In Eltan y. Alimi, Lorenzo Bosi and Chares Demetriou, eds., *The Dynamics of Radicalization*. Oxford: Oxford University Press, 24–59.

Alston, Jon P. (1989). *Wa, Guanxi*, and *Inhwa. Business Horizons* 32(2), 26–31.

Ames, Roger T. (1994). The Focus-Field Self in Classical Confuciansm. In Roger T. Ames, Wimal Dissanayake and Thomas P. Kasulis, eds., *Self as Person in Asian Theory and Practice*. Albany, NY: SUNY Press.

Ames, Roger T. (2011). *Confucian Role Ethics*. Honolulu, HI: The University of Hawai'i Press.

Ames, Roger T. and Rosemont, Henry (1998). *The Analects of Confucius*. New York: Ballantine Books.

Anker, Elisabeth (2014). Freedom and the Human. *Political Research Quarterly* 67(3), 453–456.

Ansems de Vries, Leonie (2015). *Re-imagining a politics of life: from governance of order to politics of movement*. Lanham, MD: Rowman and Littlefield.

Armstrong, David (2011). The Evolution of International Society. In John Bay-
    lis, Steve Smith and Patricia Owens, eds., *The Globalization of World Politics*.
    Oxford: Oxford University Press, 34–49.
Aron, Raymond (1973). *Peace and War*. Garden City, NY: Anchor Books.
Avelino, Flor and Rotmans, Jan (2009). Power in Transition. *European Journal of
    Social Theory* 12(4), 543–569.
Barbalet, Jack (2011). Market Relations as Wuwei. *Asian Studies Review* 35(3),
    335–354.
Barbalet, Jack (2013). Greater Self, Lesser Self. *Journal for the Theory of Social
    Behaviour* 44(2), 186–205.
Barbalet, Jack (2015). Guanxi, Tie Strength, and Network Attributes. *American
    Behavioural Scientist* 59(8), 1038–1050.
Barbalet, Jack and Qi, Xiaoying (2013). The Paradox of Power. *Journal of Political
    Power* 6(3), 405–418.
Barkin, J. Samuel (2010). *Realist constructivism: rethinking international relations
    theory*. Cambridge: Cambridge University Press.
Barzun, Jacques (1965). The Man in the American Mask. *Foreign Affairs* 43(3),
    426–435.
Baumgartner, Tom, Buckley, William and Burns, Tom R. (1975). Relational Con-
    trol. *Journal of Conflict Resolution* 19(3), 417–440.
Bell, Duran (2000). Guanxi. *Current Anthropology* 41(1), 132–138.
Bergson, Henri (2005). *Creative Evolution*. New York: Cosimo.
Bially-Mattern, Janice (2005). *Ordering International Politics*. London: Routledge.
Bilgin, Pinar (2008). Thinking Past "Western" IR. *Third World Quarterly* 29(1),
    5–23.
Bilgin, Pinar and L.H.M. Ling, eds. (2017). *Asia in international relations: unlearn-
    ing imperial power relations*. London. Routledge.
Blanchot, Maurice (1995). *The Writing of Disaster*. Lincoln, NE: University of
    Nebraska Press.
Boer, Roland (2015). Savage Peoples. *The Conversation*, 12 May.
Bourdieu, Pierre (2002). Social Space and Social Power. In M. Haugaard, ed.,
    Power. Manchester: Manchester University Press, 229–244.
Bucher, Bernd (2012). Figuratonal Sociology and the Democratic Peace. *Human
    Figurations* 1(2), 1–16.
Bullen, Roger (1979). France and Europe. In Alan Sked, ed., *Europe's Balance of
    Power*. Basingstoke: Palgrave Macmillan, 122–144.
Carlson, Allen (2010). Moving Beyond Sovereignty. *Journal of Contemporary
    China* 20(68), 89–102.
Cesa, Marco (2014). *Machiavelli on International Relations*. Oxford: Oxford Uni-
    versity Press.
Césaire, Aimé [1956] (2010). Letter to Maurice Thorez. *Social Text* 28(2), 145–152.
Cha, A. S. (1982). *The Unity of Knowledge and Action*. Honolulu, HI: University of
    Hawai'i Press.
Chalus, Elaine (2000). Elite Women, Social Politics, and the Political World. *His-
    torical Journal* 43(3), 669–697.
Chan, Joseph (2008). Territorial Boundaries and Confucianism. In Daniel Bell, ed.,
    Confucian Political Ethics. Princeton, NJ: Princeton University Press, 61–84.

Chan, Gerald (1999). *Chinese perspectives on international relations.* Basingstoke: Palgrave.

Chan, S., Mandaville, P.G. and Bleiker, R. (2001). *The Zen of International Relations.* Basinkstoke: Palgrave Macmillan.

Chang, Hui-Ching and Holt, G. Richard (1991). The Concept of Yuan. In Stella Ting-Toomey and Felipe Corzenny, eds., *Cross-Cultural Interpersonal Communication.* London: Sage, 28–57.

Chapman, Tim (2002). *The Congress of Vienna.* London: Routledge.

Charles, Victoria and Carl, Klaus H. (2014). *The Viennese Secession.* New York: Parkstone International.

Charmley, John (2005). *The Princess and the Politicians.* London: Viking.

Chen, Ching-Chang (2011). The Absence of Non-Western IR Theory in Asia Reconsidered. *International Relations of the Asia-Pacific* 11(1), 1–23.

Chen, Zhimin (2016). China, the EU and the Fragile World Order. *Journal of Common Market Studies* 54(4), 775–792.

Cheung, Martha P.Y. (2010). "To Translate" Means "To Exchange". *Target* 17(1), 33–45.

Cho, Young Chul (2015). Colonialism and Imperialism in the Quest for a Korean-Style IR Theory. *Cambridge Review of International Affairs* 28(4), 680–700.

Chong, Melody P.M., Fu, Ping Ping and Shang, Yu Fan (2013). Relational Power. *Chinese Management Studies* 7(1), 53–73.

Chow, Rey (1991). Violence in the Other Country. In Ann Russo, Lourdes Torres and Chandra Talpade Monaty, eds., *Third World Women.* Bloomington, IN: Indiana University Pres, 80–100.

Chowdhry, Geeta (2007). Edward Said and Contrapuntal Reading. *Millenium* 36(1), 101–116.

Chowdhry, Geeta and Rai, Shirin M. (2009). The Geographies of Exclusion and the Politics of Exclusion. *International Studies Perspectives* 10(1), 84–91.

Clark, Nigel (2011). Inhuman nature: *social life on a dynamic planet.* London: Sage.

Clark, Nigel (2014). Geo-Politics and the Disaster of the Anthropocene. *Sociological Review* 62(1), 19–37.

Coe, Andrew (2009). *Chop Suey.* Oxford: Oxford University Press.

Coles, Romand (2016). *Visionary Pragmatism.* Durham, NC: Duke University Press.

Cooper, Duff (2010). *Talleyrand.* London: Vintage Books.

Costa, Claudia de Lima (2013). Equivocation, Translation, and Performative Intersectionality. *Revista Anglo Saxonica* 3(6), 64–86.

Crawford, R.M.A. and Jarvis, D.S.L. (2001). *International Relations.* Albany, NY: SUNY Press.

Cromwell, Judith Lissaner (2007). *Dorothea Lieven.* Jefferson, NC: McFarland & Co.

Cudworth, Erika, Stephen Hobden, and Emilian Kavalski (2018). Framing the *posthuman dialogues in international relations.* In Erika Cudworth, Stephen Hobden, and Emilian Kavalski, eds., *Posthuman dialogues in international relations.* London: Routledge, 1–14.

de La Garde-Chambonas (August, 1902). *Anecdotal Recollections of the Congress of Vienna.* London: Chapman and Hall, Limited.

de Pradt, Dominique Georges Frédéric (1816). *The Congress of Vienna.* London: Samuel Leigh.

DeGlopper, Donald R. (1995). *Lukang*. Albany, NY: SUNY Press.

Deng, Yong (2008). *China's Struggle for Status*. Cambridge: Cambridge University Press.

Dewey, John and Bentley, Arthur (1949). *Knowing and the Known*. Boston, MA: Beacon Press.

Dirlik, Arif (2012). The idea of a 'Chinese Model'. *China Information* 26 (3), 277–302.

Donnelly, Jack (2006). Sovereign Inequalities. *European Journal of International Relations* 12(2), 133–150.

Dunne, John S. (1959). Realpolitik and the decline of the west. *The Review of Politics* 21 (1), 131–150.

Dunfee Thomas W. and Warren, Danielle E. (2001). Is Guanxi Ethical? A Normative Analysis of Doing Business in China. *Journal of Business Ethics* 32(1), 191–204.

Earnest, David C. (2015). *Massively Parallel Globalization*. Albany, NY: SUNY Press.

Elrod, Richard B (1976). The Concert of Europe: A Fresh Look at an International System. *World Politics* 28 (2), 159–174.

Elson Roessler, Shirley and Miklos, Reny (2003). *Europe 1715–1919*. Lanham, MD: Rowman and Littlefield.

Emirbayer, Mustafa (1997). Manifesto for a relational sociology. *American Journal of Sociology* 103 (2), 281–317.

Emirbayer, Mustafa and Mische, Ann (1998). What Is Agency? *American Journal of Sociology* 103(4), 962–1023.

Enloe, Cynthia (1989). *Bananas, Beaches, and Bases*. Berkeley, CA: University of California Press.

Eun, Young-Soo (2016). *Pluralism and Engagement*. Basingstoke: Palgrave Macmillan.

Farh, Jiing-Lih, Tsui, Anne S., Xin, Katherine and Cheng, Bor-Shiuan (1998). The Influence of Relational Demography and Guanxi. *Organization Science* 9(4), 471–488.

Field, David Dudley (1884). *Speeches*. New York: Appleton & Co.

Frisina, Warren G. (1982). *The Unity of Knowledge and Action*. Honolulu, HI: University of Hawai'i Press.

Ford, Christopher (2010). *Mind of Empire*. Lexington, KY: University Press of Kentucky.

Foucault, Michel [1973] (2002). *The Order of Things*. London: Routledge.

Gao, Yanli (2008). China's World View. *Dimensioni e problemi della ricerca storica* 20(1), 255–268.

Geertz, Clifford (1998). Deep Hanging Out. *The New York Review of Books*, 22 October.

Gilpin, Robert (1981). *War and Change in World Politics*. Cambridge: Cambridge University Press.

Gold, Thomas, Ghine, Dong and Wank, David L. (2002). *Social Connections in China*. Cambridge: Cambridge University Press.

Gottlieb, Gideon A.G. (1983). Relationalism. *University of Chicago Law Review* 50(3), 567–612.

Gottmann, Jean (1952). The Political Partioning of Our World. *World Politics* 4(4), 512–519.

Graig, Gordon Alexander (1972). *Europe, 1815–1914.* New York: Holt, Rinehart and Winston.

Gress, David (1998). *From Plato to NATO.* New York: The Free Press.

Grubb, Kenneth Goerge (1957). *Coexistence and the Conditions of Peace.* London: S. C. M. Press.

Gulick, Edward V. (1955). *Europe's Classical Balance of Power.* New York: Norton.

Guo Rui (2008). On Balance of Power. *Journal of Jiangnan Social University* 16 (1), 1–16.

Hammond, Scott C. and Glenn, Lowell M. (2004). The Ancient Practice of Chinese Social Networking: Guanxi and Social Network Theory. *Emergence Complexity and Organization* 6(1/2), 24–31.

Harnisch, S., Bersick, S. and Gottwald, J-C., eds. (2016). *China's International Roles.* London: Routledge.

Haukkala, Hiski (2008). A norm-maker or a norm-taker? The changing normative parameters of Russia's place in Europe. In Ted Hopf, ed. *Russia's European Choice.* Basingstoke: Palgrave Macmillan, 35–58.

Heffner, Lanette (2008). *Inside the Dragon's Briefcase.* San Antonio, TX: University of Texas.

Hegel, Georg W.F. (1995). *Lectures on the History of Philosophy.* Lincoln, NE: University of Nebraska Press.

Held, David (2004). *A Globalizing World?* London: Routledge.

Heng, Yee-Kuang (2010). Ghosts in the Machine. *International Relations* 47(5), 535–556.

Hinsley, Francis Harry (1963). *Power and the Pursuit of Peace.* Cambridge: Cambridge University Press.

Ho, David Y.F. (1976). On the Concept of Face. *American Journal of Sociology* 81(4), 867–884.

Ho, David Y.F. (1995). Selfhood and Identity. *Journal of the Theory of Social Behaviour* 25(2), 115–139.

Hobson, John M. (2004). *The Eastern Origins of Western Civilisation.* Cambridge: Cambridge University Press.

Hobson, John M. (2012). *The Eurocentric Conception of World Politics.* Cambridge: Cambridge University Press.

Hoffman, Ross (1941). *The great republic: a historical view of the international community and the organization of peace.* New York: Sheed & Ward.

Holdbraad, Carsten (1970). *The Concert of Europe.* Upper Saddle River, NJ: Prentice Hall Press.

Holdbraad, Carsten (1971). The Concert of Europe. *Australian Outlook* 25(1), 29–44.

Holdbraad, Carsten (1979). *Superpowers and International Conflict.* London: Palgrave Macmillan.

Holdbraad, Carsten (1984). *Middle Powers in International Politics.* London: Palgrave Macmillan.

Holsti, Kalevi J. (1992). Governance Without Government. In James N. Rosenau and Ernst-Otto Czempiel, eds., *Governance Without Government*. Cambridge: Cambridge University Press, 30–57.

Horesh, Niv and Emilian Kavalski, eds. (2014). *Asian thought on China's changing international relations*. Basingstoke: Palgrave.

Howard, Michael (2000). *The Invention of Peace*. New Haven, CT: Yale University Press.

Hückel, Bettina (2012). Theory of International Relations With Chinese Characteristics. *Diskurs* 8(2), 34–64.

Huang, Chiung-Chiu and Chih-yu Shih (2014). *Harmonious intervention: China's quest for relational security*. London: Routledge.

Hurrel, Andrew (2007). *On Global Order*. Oxford: Oxford University Press.

Hutchings, Kimberly (2008). *Time and World Politics*. Manchester: Manchester University Press.

Hwang, Kwang-kuo (1987). Face and Favour. *American Journal of Sociology* 92(4), 944–974.

Jackson, Patrick Thaddeus and Nexon, Daniel (1999). Relations Before States. *European Journal of International Relations* 5(3), 291–332.

Jackson, Patrick Thaddeus and Nexon, Daniel (2017). Reclaiming the Social, presented at the workshop, 'Futures of Global Relationality', Lancaster University, 16–17 May.

Jarrett, Mark (2013). *The Congress of Vienna and Its Legacy*. London: I.B. Tauris.

Jervis, Robert (1986). From Balance to Concert. In Kenneth A. Oye, ed., *Cooperation Under Anarchy*. Princeton, NJ: Princeton University Press, 58–79.

Jia, Wenshan (2006). The *Wei – Ming – Lianmian – Guanxi – Renqing* – Complex. In Peter H. Hershock and Roger T. Ames, eds., *Confucian Cultures of Authority*. Albany, NY: SUNY Press, 49–64.

Jia, Wenshan (2009). An Intercultural Communication Model of IR. In Yufan Hao, C.X. George Wei and Lowell Dittmer, eds., *Challenges to Chinese Foreign Policy*. Lexington, KY: University Press of Kentucky, 319–334.

Jørgensen, Knud Erik and Wong, Reuben (2016). Social Constructivist Perspectives on China-EU Relations. In Jianwei Wang and Weiqing Song, eds., *China, the European Union*. Basingstoke: Palgrave Macmillan, 51–76.

Kagan, Korina (1997). The myth of the European concert: The realist-institutionalist debate and great power behavior in the eastern question, 1821–41, *Security Studies* 7 (2), 1–57.

Kant, Immanuel (1991). *Political Writings*. Cambridge: Cambridge University Press.

Katzenstein, Peter J. (2010). A World of Plural and Pluralistic Civilizations. In Peter J. Katzenstein, ed., *Civilizations in World Politics*. London: Routledge, 1–40.

Kavalski, Emilian (2007). The Fifth Debate and the Emergence of Complex International Relations Theory: Notes on the Application of Complexity Theory to the Study of International Life. *Cambridge Review of International Affairs* 20(3), 435–454.

Kavalski, Emilian (2008). The Complexity of Global Security Governance: An Analytical Overview. *Global Society* 22(4), 423–443.

Kavalski, Emilian (2009). Timescapes of Security: Clocks, Clouds, and the Complexity of Security Governance. *World Futures* 65(7), 527–551.

Kavalski, Emilian (2011). From the Cold War to Global Warming: Observing Complexity in IR. *Political Studies Review* 9(1), 1–12.

Kavalski, Emilian (2012). *Central Asia and the Rise of Normative Powers: Contextualizing the Security Governance of the European Union, China, and India.* New York: Bloomsbury.

Kavalski, Emilian (2013). The Struggle for Recognition of Normative Powers: Normative Power Europe and Normative Power China in Context. *Cooperation and Conflict* 48(2), 247–267.

Kavalski, Emilian (2015). *World Politics at the Edge of Chaos: Reflections on Complexity and Global Life.* Albany, NY: State University of New York Press.

Kavalski, Emilian (2016). Relationality and Its Chinese Characteristics. *China Quarterly* 226, 551–559.

Kavalski, Emilian (2017). Whether Power Transition and Whither If One. In David Walton and Emilian Kavalski, eds., *Power Transition in Asia.* London: Routledge, 207–221.

Kavalski, Emilian (2018a). The Normative Dimension of EU-China Relations: Acquis Communautaire vs Guanxi. In Sebastian Bersick, Kerry Brown, Andrew Cottey, Jörn-Carsten Gottwald and Wei Shen, eds., *Routledge Handbook on EU-China Relations.* London: Routledge.

Kavalski, Emilian (2018b). Complexity thinking and the relational ethics of global life. In Birgit Schippers, ed. *The Routledge Handbook to Rethinking Ethics in International Relations.* London: Routledge, 123–141.

Kavalski, Emilian and Chul Cho, Young (2015). Governing Uncertainty in Turbulent Times. *Comparative Sociology* 14(3), 429–444.

Kavalski, Emilian and Zolkos, Magdalena (2016). The Recognition of Nature in International Relations. In Patrick Hayden and Kate Schick, eds., *Recognition and Global Politics.* Manchester: Manchester University Press, 139–156.

Kavalski, Emilian, Stephen Hobden and Erika Cudworth (2018). Beyond the anthropocentric partitioning of the world. In Erika Cudworth, Stephen Hobden, and Emilian Kavalski, eds., *Posthuman dialogues in international relations.* London: Routledge, 277–290.

King, Ambrose Y.C. (1985). The Individual and Group in Confucianism. In Donald J. Munro, ed., *Individualism and Holism.* Ann Arbor, MI: University of Michigan Press, 57–72.

Kipnis, Andrew (1997). *Producing Guanxi.* Durham, NC: Duke University Press.

Kissinger, Henry (1957). *A World Restored.* Boston, MA: Houghton Mifflin.

Kissinger, Henry (2011). *On China.* New York: Allan Lane.

Kompridis, Nikolas (2006). *Critique and Disclosure.* Cambridge, MA: MIT Press.

Kowalzig, Barbara (2005). Performances of *Theoria.* In Jas Elsner and Ian Rutherford, eds., *Pilgrimage in Graeco-Roman and Early Christian Antiquity.* Oxford: Oxford University Press, 41–72.

Krasner, Stephen (1983). Structural Causes and Regime Consequences. In Stephen D. Krasner, ed., *International Regimes.* Ithaca, NY: Cornell University Press, 1–21.

Kratochwil, Friedrich and Ruggie, Joh Gerard (1986). International Organization. *International Organization* 40(4), 753–775.

Krippendorf, Klaus (2000). Ecological Narratives. In Jose V. Ciprut, ed., *The Art of the Feud: Reconceptualising International Relations*. Westport, CT: Praeger, 1–19.

Krishna, Sankaran (2001). Race, Amnesia, and the Education of International Relations. *Alternatives* 26(1), 401–424.

Kurki, Miljia (2008). *Causation in International Relations*. Cambridge: Cambridge University Press.

Lai, Karyn L. (2008). *An Introduction to Chinese Philosophy*. Cambridge: Cambridge University Press.

Landes, Joan (2008). *Women and the Political Sphere*. Ithaca, NY: Cornell University Press.

Langenberg, Eike A. (2007). *Guanxi and Business Strategy*. New York: Springer.

Lascurettes, Kyle (2017). The Concert of Europe and Great-Power Governance Today. *RAND Perspective*, No. 226.

Lasswell, Harold (1935). *World Politics and Personal Insecurity*. New York: The Free Press.

Lasswell, Harold (1936). *Politics: Who Gets What, When, and How*. New York: Whittlesey House.

Lasswell, Harold (1948). *Power and Personality*. New York: W. W. Norton & Co.

Lau, D.C. (1979). *The Analects*. London: Penguin Press.

Lauren, Paul Gordon (1983). Crisis Prevention in Nineteenth-Century Diplomacy. In Alexander George, ed., *Managing US-Soviet Rivalry*. Boulder, CO: Westview Press, 31–64.

Lebow, Richard Ned (2003). *The Tragic Vision of World Politics*. Cambridge: Cambridge University Press.

Ledeneva, Alena (2008). 'Blat' and 'Guanxi'. *Comparative Studies in Society and History* 50(1), 118–144.

Lee, Don Y. and Dawes, Philip L. (2005). Guanxi, Trust, and Long-Term Orientation. *Journal of International Marketing* 13(2), 28–56.

Ling, L.H.M. (2015). *The Dao of World Politics*. London: Routledge.

Liu, Jee Loo (2011). Reconstructing Chinese Metaphysics. *Journal of East-West Thought* 1(2), 1–13.

Liu, Qing (2014). From 'All Under Heaven' to Critical Cosmopolitanism. In Candido Mendes, ed., *Shared Values in a World of Cultural Pluralism*. Rio de Janeiro: Academy of Latinity, 119–148.

Loke, B. (2010). Between interest and responsibility: assessing China's foreign policy and burgeoning global role. *Asian Security* 5 (3), 195–215.

Luo, Yadong (1997). Guanxi. *Human Systems Management* 16(1), 43–51.

Lyon, Peter (1970). The Great Globe Itself. In Peter Lyon and Edith Penrose, eds., *New Orientations*. London: Frank Cass & Co, 1–27.

Mancall, Mark (1984). *China at the Center: 300 Years of Foreign Policy*. New York: The Free Press.

Manners, Ian (2002). Normative power Europe: a contradiction in terms? *Journal of Common Market Studies* 40 (2), 235–258.

Mastnak, Tomaž (2003). Europe and the Muslims. In Emran Qureshi and Michael A. Sells, eds., *The New Crusades*. New York: Columbia University Press, 205–248.

Matzka, Manfred (2015). 1815: The Idea of Europe. *Austrian Information*, 1 November.

Mazower, Mark (2013). *Governing the World*. New York: Penguin Books.

Medhurst, W.H. (1838). *China*. London: John Snow.

Medlicott, W.N. (1956). *Bismarck, Gladstone, and the Concert of Europe*. London: Athlone Press.

Mierhofer, Waltrand, Riesch, Gertrud and Bland, Caroline, eds. (2008). *Women Against Napoleon*. Frankfurt am Main: Campus Verlag.

Mische, Ann (2011). Relational Sociology, Culture and Agency. In John Scott and Peter Carrington, eds., *The Sage Handbook of Social Network Analysis*. Thousand Oaks, CA: Sage, 80–89.

Mitzen, Jennifer (2005). Reading Habermas in Anarchy: Multilateral Diplomacy and Global Public Spheres. *American Political Science Review* 99 (3), 401–417.

Mitzen, Jennifer (2013). *Power in Concert*. Chicago, IL: University of Chicago Press.

Moisi, Dominique (2014). The Congress of Vienna Revisited. *Project Syndicate*, 25 September.

Morefield, Jeanne (2014). *Empires Without Imperialism*. Oxford: Oxford University Press.

Morgenthau, Hans J. (1948). *Politics Among Nations*. New York: Alfred A. Knopf.

Morgenthau, Hans J. (1958). *Dilemmas of Politics*. Chicago, IL: University of Chicago Press.

Mowat, R.B. (1930). *The Concert of Europe*. London: Palgrave Macmillan.

Murphy, Cornelius F. (1985). *The Search for World Order*. Dordrecht: Martinus Nijhoff Publishers.

Nel, Philip (2010). Redistribution and recognition: what emerging regional powers want. *Review of International Studies* 36 (4), 951–974.

Nexon, Daniel H. (2009). *The Struggle for Power in Early Modern Europe*. Princeton, NJ: Princeton University Press.

Nichols, Irby C. (1971). *The European Pentarchy and the Congress of Verona*. The Hague: Martinus Nijhoff.

Nicolson, Harold (1946). *The Congress of Vienna*. New York: Harold, Brace and Co.

Nightingale, Andrea Wilson (2004). *Spectacles of Truth in Classical Greek Philosophy*. Cambridge: Cambridge University Press.

Nordin, Astrid H.M. (2015). Hegemony in Chinese? In Lion König and Bidisha Chaudhuri, eds., *Politics of the 'Other' in India and China*. London: Routledge, 206–216.

Nordin, Astrid H.M. (2016). *China's International Relations and Harmonious World*. London: Routledge.

Odysseos, Louiza (2007). *The Subject of Coexistence*. Minneapolis, MN: University of Minnesota Press.

Osiander, Andreas (1994). *The States System of Europe*. Oxford: Clarendon Press.

Paltiel, Jeremy (2009). China's Regionalization Policies. In Emilian Kavalski, ed., *China and the Global Politics of Regionalization*. Abingdon: Routledge, 47–62.

Pan, Chengxin (2013). *Knowledge, Desire, and Power in Global Politics*. London: Edward Elgar.

Pan, Zhongqi (2016). Guanxi, Weiqi and Chinese Strategic Thinking. *Chinese Political Science Review* 1(1), 303–321.

Parks, Malcolm R. (1982). Ideology of Interpersonal Communication. In Michael Burgon, ed., *Communication Yearbook*. New Brunswick, NJ: Transaction Publishers, 79–107.

Patomäki, Haikki (2002). *After International Relations*. London: Routledge.

Peterson, Genevive (1945). Political inequality and the congress of Vienna. *Political Science Quarterly* 60 (4), 532–554.

Pillalamarri, Akhilesh (2016). The Five Most Important Treaties in World History. *The National Interest*, 12 November.

Protevi, Jon (2013). *Life, War, Earth*. Minneapolis, MN: University of Minnesota Press.

Pye, Lucian W. (1968). *The Spirit of Chinese Politics*. Cambridge, MA: MIT Press.

Pye, Lucian W. (1982). *Chinese Commercial Negotiating Style*. Cambridge, MA: Oelgeschlager, Guun and Hain.

Pye, Lucian W. (1995). Factions and the Politics of Guanxi. *The China Journal* 34(2), 35–53.

Qin, Yaqing (2007). Why Is There No Chinese International Theory. *International Relations of the Asia-Pacific* 7(3), 313–340.

Qin Yaqing (2009). Relationality and Processual Construction. *Social Sciences in China* 30(3), 5–20.

Qin Yaqing (2011). Rule, Rules, and Relations. *Chinese Journal of International Politics* 3(2), 129–153.

Qin Yaqing (2016). A Relational Theory of World Politics. *International Studies Perspectives* 18(1), 22–47.

Qin Yaqing (2017). Representaion Is Practice, presented at the workshop, 'Futures of Global Relationality', Lancaster University, 16–17 May.

Querejazu, Amaya (2016). Encountering the pluriverse: looking for alternatives in other worlds. *Revista Brasileira de Politica Intrnacional* 59(2), 1–16.

Ramel, Frédéric (2014). Perpetual Peace. In Rebekah Ahrendt, Mark Ferragute and Damien Mahiet, eds., *Music and Diplomacy*. Basingstoke: Palgrave Macmillan, 125–145.

Rendall, Matthew (2000). Russia, the Concert of Europe, and Greece. *Security Studies* 9(4), 52–90.

Reus-Smit, Christian (1999). *The Moral Purpose of the State*. Princeton, NJ: Princeton University Press.

Reinsch, Paul S. (1900). *World politics at the end of the nineteenth century: as influenced by the oriental situation*. New York: Macmillan and Co.

Richardson, James L. (1994). *Crisis Diplomacy*. Cambridge: Cambridge University Press.

Richardson, L.F. (1956). Mathematics of War. In James R. Newman, ed., *The World of Mathematics*. New York: Simon and Schuster, 1240–1253.

Richardson, Sarah (2013). *The Political World of Women*. London: Routledge.

Risse, Thomas (2000). Let's Argue. *International Organization* 54(1), 1–39.

Rojas, Cristina (2016). Contesting the Colonial. *International Political Sociology* 10(2), 369–382.

Rosecrance, Richard N., ed. (2001). *The New Great Power Coalition*. Lanham, MD: Rowman & Littlefield.

Rosemont, Henry (1991). Rights-Bearing Individuals and Role-Bearing Persons. In Mary I. Bockover, ed., *Rules, Rituals, Responsibilities*. La Salle, IL: Open Court.

Rosemont, Henry (2006). Two Loci of Authority. In Peter H. Hershock and Roger T. Ames, eds., *Confucian Cultures of Authority*. Albany, NY: SUNY Press, 1–20.

Rosenau, James N. (1990). *Turbulence in World Politics*. Princeton, NJ: Princeton University Press.

Russell, Roberto and Tokatlian, Juan Gabriel (2003). From Antagonistic Autonomy to Relational Autonomy. *Latin American Politics and Society* 45(1), 1–24.

Sahlins, Marshall (1972). *Stone Age Economics*. Chicago, IL: Aldine-Atherton Inc.

Satow, Ernest (1925). *Pacta sunt servanda* or International Guarantee. *Cambridge Historical Journal* 1(3), 295–318.

Schenk, H.G. (1947). *The Aftermath of the Napoleonic Wars*. New York: Routledge & Kegan Paul, Trench, Trubner and Co.

Schnitzler, Henry (1954). 'Gay Vienna' – myth and reality. *Journal of the History of Ideas* 15 (1), 94–118.

Schroeder, Paul W. (1983). Containment Nineteenth Century Style. *South Atlantic Quarterly* 15(1), 1–18.

Schroeder, Paul W. (1992). Did the Vienna Settlement Rest on a Balance of Power. *The American Historical Review* 93(3), 683–706.

Schroeder, Paul W. (1994). *The Transformation of European Politics*. New York: Oxford University Press.

Schulz, Matthias (2007). Did Norms Matter? In Holger Afflerbach and David Stevenson, eds., *An Improbable War*. New York: Berghahn Books, 43–61.

Schwartz, Benjamin I. (1967). The Maoist Image of World Order. *Journal of International Affairs* 21 (1), 73–98.

Setton-Watson, R.W. (1955). *Britain in Europe*. Cambridge: Cambridge University Press.

Shahi, Deepshikha and Ascione, Gennaro (2016). Rethinking the Absence of Post-Western International Relations Theory in India. *European Journal of International Relations* 22(2), 313–334.

Shen, V. (1994). Structure, Meaning, and Critique. In Ching-Sung Shen, Richard Knwoles and Van Doan Tran, eds., *Psychology, Phenomenology, and Chinese Philosophy*. Washington, DC: CRVP, 167–176.

Shih, Chih-yu (2013). *Sinicizing International Relations*. Basingstoke: Palgrave Macmillan.

Shih, Chih-yu (2016). Affirmative Balance. *International Studies Perspectives*, 1–21.

Shilliam, Robbie (2010). *International Relations and Non-Western Thought*. New York: Routledge.

Shimizu, Kosuke (2013). Who Owns Our Tongue? *ARC Working Paper Series* No. 21.

Shimizu, Kosuke (2015). Materializing the Non-Western. *Cambridge Review of International Affairs* 28(1), 3–20.

Shorske, Carl E. (1961). *Fin-de-siècle Vienna*. New York: Vintage Books.

Simpson, Gerry (2004). *Great Powers and Outlaw States*. Cambridge: Cambridge University Press.

Sinsheimer, Max P. (2016). The Congress of Vienna. In Catherine Donnelly, ed., *The Oxford Companion to Cheese*. Oxford: Oxford University Press, 185–186.

Slantchev, Branislav L. (2005). Territory and commitment: The concert of Europe as self-enforcing equilibrium. *Security Studies* 14 (4), 565–606.

Sluga, Glenda (2014). Sexual Congress. *History Today* 64(9), 33–39.

Sluga, Glenda and James, Carolyn, eds. (2015). *Women, International Politics, and Diplomacy*. London: Routledge.

Strong, George V. (1987). Review of *The Congress Dances: Vienna 1814–1815*. *History of European Ideas* 8 (1), 103–104.

Solomon, Richard H. (1975). *A Revolution Is Not a Dinner Party*. New York: Anchor Books.

Solomon, Richard H. (1995). *Chinese Political Negotiating Behaviour*. Santa Monica, CA: Rand.

Soutou, Georges-Henri (2000). Was There a European Order in the Twentieth Century? *Contemporary European History* 9(3), 329–353.

Spiel, Hilde, ed. (1968). *The Congress of Vienna*. Philadelphia, PA: Chilton Book Co.

Su, Chenting and Littlefield, James E. (2001). Entering Guanxi. *Journal of Business Ethics* 3(3), 199–210.

Swaine, Margaret Byrne (2013). Chinese Cosmopolitanism. In Tami Blumenfield and Helaine Silverman, eds., *Cultural Heritage Politics in China*. New York: Springer, 33–50.

Tan, Doreen and Snell, Robin Stanley (2002). The third eye: exploring guanxi and relational morality. *Journal of Business Ethics* 41(2), 361–384.

Taylor, Alan J.P. (1954). *The Struggle for Mastery in Europe*. Oxford: Oxford University Press.

Teschke, Bruno (2003). *The Myth of 1648*. London: Verso.

Thacker, Eugene (2009). The Shadows of Atheology. *Theory, Culture, & Society* 26(6), 134–152.

Todorov, Tzvetan (1982). *The Conquest of America*. New York: Harper & Row.

Tong, Shijun (2006). Chinese Thought and Dialogical Universalism. In Gerard Delanty, ed., *Europe and Asia Beyond East and West*. London: Routledge, 305–315.

Tsui, Anne S. and Farh, Jiing-Lih Larry (1997). Where Guanxi Matters. *Work and Occupations* 24(1), 56–79.

Tu, Wei-Ming (1985). *Confucian Thought*. Albany, NY: SUNY Press.

Uemura, Takeshi (2015). Understanding Chinese Foreign Relations. *International Studies Perspectives* 16(3), 345–365.

Vick, Brian E. (2014). *The Congress of Vienna*. Cambridge, MA: Harvard University Press.

Viotti, Paul R. and Kauppi, Mark V. (2013). *International Relations and World Politics*. Boston, MA: Pearson.

Vucetic, Srdjan (2011). *The Anglosphere*. Stanford, CA: Stanford University Press.

Walker, Anne Collins (2012). *China Calls*. Lanham, MD: Rowman & Littlefield.

Waltz, Kenneth N. (1979). *Theory of International Politics.* Boston, MA: Addison-Wesley.

Waltz, Kenneth N. (2002). The continuity of international politics. In Ken Booth and Tim Dunne (eds), *Worlds in Collision.* Basingstoke: Palgrave Macmillan, 44–79.

Watson, Adam (1985). Russia and the European State System. In Hedley Bull and Adam Watson, eds., *The Expansion of International Society.* Oxford: Clarendon Press, 61–74.

Watson, Adam (1987). *The Evolution of International Society.* London: Routledge.

Weakland, John H. (1950). The Organization of Action in Chinese Culture. *Psychology* 13(3), 361–370.

Webster, Charles K. (1934). *The Foreign Policy of Castlreagh.* London: G. Bell.

Weitz, Eric D. (2008). From the Vienna to the Paris System. *The American Historical Review* 113(5), 1313–1343.

Welch, Ellen R. (2017). *A Theatre of Diplomacy.* Philadelphia, PA: University of Pennsylvania Press.

Wellman, Barry (1998). Structural Analysis. In Barry Wellman and S. D. Berkowitz, eds., *Social Structures.* Cambridge: Cambridge University Press, 19–61.

Wen, Haiming and Wang, Hang (2013). Confucian Cultural Psychology. *Culture & Psychology* 19(2), 184–202.

Whitman, Jim (2005). *The limits of global governance* (London: Routledge).

Whyte, Jessica (2017). Subjectivism and the Standard of Living, paper presented at the workshop 'Happiness in Neoliberalist', University of New South Wales, 10 March.

Wieland, Christian (2012). The Consequences of Early Modern Diplomacy. In Antje Flichter and Susan Richter, eds., *Structures on the Move.* New York: Springer, 271–285.

Wight, Martin (1960). Why Is There No International Theory? *International Relations* 2(1), 35–48, 62.

Wight, Martin (1977). *Systems of States.* Leicester: Leicester University Press.

Wolfers, Arnold (1962). *Discord and Collaboration.* Baltimore, NJ: The John Hopkins University Press.

Womack, Brantly (2008). China as a normative foreign policy actor. In Natali Tocci, ed. *Who is a normative foreign policy actor? The European Union and its global partners.* Brussels: Centre for European Policy Studies, 265–300.

Wong, David (2004). Relational and Autonomous Selves. *Journal of Chinese Philosophy* 31(4), 420–421.

Wong, Reuben (2013). The Issue of Identity in the EU-China Relationship. *Politique Européene* 39(1), 1580185.

Yang, K.S. and Ho, David Y.F. (1988). The Role of Yuan. In Anand C. Paranjpe, David Y.F. Ho and Robert W. Rieber, eds., *Asian Contributions to Psychology.* New York: Praeger, 263–281.

Yang, Mayfair Mei-hui (1994). *Gifts, Favors, and Banquets.* Ithaca, NY: Cornell University Press.

Yang, Mayfair Mei-hui (2002). The Resilience of Guanxi. *The China Quarterly* 42(170), 459–476.

Yeung, Irene Y.M. and Tung, Rosalie L. (1996). Achieving Success in Confucian Societies. *Organizational Dynamics* 25(2), 54–65.

Yu, P.K.H. (2012). *International Governance and Regimes*. London: Routledge.

Yue, Ricky Wai-kay (2015). Beyond Dependency. *Bandung* 2(4), 1–17.

Yurdusev, A. Nuri (2003). *International Relations*. Basingstoke: Palgrave Macmillan.

Zamoyski, Adam (2001). *Rites of Peace*. London: HarperCollins.

Zhang, Feng (2015). Confucian Foreign Policy. *Chinese Journal of International Politics* 8(2), 197–218.

Zhang, Feng (2016). *Chinese Hegemony*. Stanford, CA: Stanford University Press.

Zhang, Yongjin (2017). China and Liberal Hierarchies. *International Affairs* 92(4), 798–816.

Zhao, Tingyang (2006). Rethinking Empire. *Social Identities* 12(1), 29–41.

Zhao, Tingyang (2009). A Political World. *Diogenes* 56(5), 5–18.

Zhao Tingyang (2012). 'All-Under-Heaven and methodological relationalism'. In Fred Dallmayr and Zhao Tingyang, eds. *Contemporary Chinese Political Thought: Debates and Perspectives*. Lexington, KT: University Press of Kentucky.

Zhao, Tingyang (2015). How to Make a World. In Johanna Sebt and Jesper Garsdal, eds., *How Is Global Dialogue Possible?* Berlin: Walter de Gruyter, 289–307.

Index

For Product Safety Concerns and Information please contact our EU
representative GPSR@taylorandfrancis.com
Taylor & Francis Verlag GmbH, Kaufingerstraße 24, 80331 München, Germany

www.ingramcontent.com/pod-product-compliance
Ingram Content Group UK Ltd.
Pitfield, Milton Keynes, MK11 3LW, UK
UKHW021423080625
459435UK00011B/128